THE ODES
AND EPODES
OF HORACE

"Better a live Sparrow than a stuffed Eagle."
EDWARD FITZGERALD

THE ODES
AND EPODES
OF HORACE

A Modern English Verse Translation
by
JOSEPH P. CLANCY

THE UNIVERSITY OF CHICAGO PRESS
CHICAGO & LONDON

To My Mother and Father

THE UNIVERSITY OF CHICAGO PRESS, CHICAGO 60637
The University of Chicago Press, Ltd., London

Published 1960. Printed in the United States of America

04 03 02 01 00 99 98 97 96 95   11 12 13 14 15

ISBN: 0–226–10679–9 (paperbound)
LCN: 60–16059

This book is printed on acid-free paper.

CONTENTS

GENERAL INTRODUCTION

In or about 23 B.C., the first three books of *Carmina* by Quintus Horatius Flaccus were published. The author of these lyrics—they are more frequently, and less accurately, called odes—was then forty-two years old. He was secure in the favor of the emperor Augustus and in the patronage of the nobleman Maecenas; he was comfortable on his Sabine Farm, Maecenas' gift, where he could live as a country gentleman, with all the time he needed to study and write; he was certain of his poetic gift and accomplishment. All this is reflected in his lyrics; the experience of contentment is vital to many of them. But Horace had lived through three major political crises in a society refined but beginning to rot, and this, too, plays its part in the poems.

Horace's father was a freedman of Venusia, in southeastern Italy. It is to his concern for his son that we owe the poems, for Horace tells us (*Satires* i. 6) how his father brought him to Rome for his education and how he devoted himself to the boy's welfare. Horace was a student at Rome when Julius Caesar defied the Senate and crossed the Rubicon, defeated Pompey (48 B.C.), and assumed control of the state. At the age of nineteen, Horace went to Athens for further study. Grammar, rhetoric, and philosophy were the bases of Roman education: the mark of his rhetorical training is everywhere in Horace, sometimes, one feels, too obtrusively present, as in *Odes* ii. 9; he is no Lucretius, but both the Stoic concept of virtue and the Epicurean concept of happiness affect his life and poetry. We may presume that by his twenty-first year he had read widely in Greek poetry and was aware of his own calling. But in that year Julius Caesar was assassinated, and Brutus came to Athens.

Horace joined the cause of Roman republicanism and the army of Brutus. Both were defeated at Philippi in 42 B.C. Horace's father had died, and his inheritance was confiscated by Octavian. But the following year Octavian granted a general amnesty: Horace returned to Rome, gained clerical work, and began to write verse. His friendship with other poets, including Vergil, resulted in his introduction to Maecenas, Octavian's friend and adviser. Thereafter things went well: Horace moved in the high society of his time, on intimate terms with generals, public officials, patrons of the arts, and Octavian himself. No one could have been more grateful, or less servile: his relations with Maecenas were those of friend to friend, not servant to master; he is said to have refused the post of private secretary to Octavian.

When a new civil war broke out between Octavian and Antony, Horace was firmly on Octavian's side. After 30 B.C. Octavian, who took the name of Augustus in 27 B.C.,[1] was sole ruler of the empire. That Horace frequently wrote what Augustus liked to hear is undeniable; but we should be wary of charging his political poems with insincerity, as there is some difference between good sense and sycophancy. Horace seems to have recognized that, whatever his earlier political sympathies had been, the best chance for stability in the state lay with Augustus: the evidence indicates that he was right. Augustus, for all the doubtful quality of his personal and political behavior, especially in his early years, had the ideal

---

[1] In the criticism and annotation in the remainder of this book, I have referred to Octavian as Augustus regardless of the date involved.

of establishing a lasting foundation for civil peace, and Horace celebrated both the ideal and the evidences of its achievement.

No one should be foolish enough to expect consistency of a lyric poet, but the several voices we hear in reading Horace are worth our attention. The poet who protests that he is only a "poet of parties" assumes at other times the role of a prophetic bard; singing of the joys of a retired life and "golden moderation," he takes part in riotous banquets and chants approval of the empire's expansion; celebrating the laws encouraging marriage and berating the sexual license of his fellow citizens, he remains a bachelor, sighs after girls and boys, and romps in verse with Lydia, Lyde, and Lalage. Several voices, and whatever the temptation to call them public and private, Roman and Greek, it is not as easy as that. Nor can we assume a chronological development, from Roman luxury to Sabine simplicity, in the composition of the lyrics, though Horace's later years seem to have been devoted to his country life. Nor is it true that one voice produces better poetry than another, though in our time we may be more comfortable with the personal than with the political poems.

The voices come from conflicting forces at the heart of Roman life itself, and the poet's imagination responds equally to contrasting experiences. The Roman ideal of the soldier-farmer, trained to a life of privation, to sacrifice his private wishes to the needs of the fatherland, to die rather than surrender: this was a noble tradition and Horace turns it into splendid poetry. The strict domestic morality of the early Romans: this too evoked admiration. Augustus' awareness of the breakdown of belief in these traditions, and his attempts to reform Roman society: Horace opens Book III of the *Odes*

with six poems on the ancestral virtues and the failure of hi
fellow citizens to live up to them, with the bitterest lines pic
turing the degeneration of ethical standards in the home. Th
glory of empire: it would have been hard for Horace not t
respond to this, to the spread of "civilization," to the feelin
that it was wonderful to be a citizen of the city that ruled th
world. But the pleasures of sex and music and wine, the amus
ing round of affairs and squabbles and parties: of this, too
poetry could be made. The surfeit and tedium in sophisticate
society, the freshness and delight of a way of life that de
manded less and gave more, that was disciplined and satis
fying: here, again, was an experience for poems. And beneatl
all these, the sad awareness of time and death, and the jo
that was highest and best, the joy of poetry.

While Horace experienced contradictions in his society an
himself and made poetry out of them, he never uses his ow
self-division as a central tension for a poem. The contrast i
between poems: it is not present in a single poem, eithe
almost unconsciously, harmful to the poem's structure, as ir
Tennyson's "Ulysses," or consciously used as the dramatic
principle of structure, as in Shakespeare's dark sonnets o
Donne's devotional poems. Horace allows each experience its
own poem and exploits the contrasts by arranging the lyrics
to show thematic variety and variations on a theme. Perhaps
it is wrong to speak of him as self-divided: the true Horatian
note is serenity, and it comes in part from accepting and
using the multiplicity of experience to create lasting art. For,
however much he was genuinely stirred by certain ethical
ideals and practiced them, however devoted he was to his
friends and to his patron, he was at the core a man who lived
for his art, preserving a certain coolness in his relations with
everyone and everything but the Muse.

4

Lyric poetry is the most difficult to translate, and that of Horace is almost impossible, as all who have tried it will testify. Harold Mattingly has remarked both the problem and its fascination: "a task almost fantastically difficult, like making ropes out of sand or translating the Odes of Horace into English"; "everyone wants to translate him."[2]

This book is intended primarily for readers with little or no Latin, but I hope it offers some pleasure to the others, those who can read an original and therefore enjoy a translator's moments of failure at least as much as his moments of triumph. Without assuming authority or success, or presuming to set down principles for translation, I wish to indicate what I have attempted and not attempted to do.

The negative first: what cannot be done, at least by me.

Horace prided himself on being the first to "adapt Aeolian song to Italian verses," to use Greek lyric meters for Latin poems.[3] Catullus had, it is true, attempted this in several poems; but the four books of Horace's lyrics represent a major and difficult technical achievement, and one that later Latin poets did not follow. The meters of Greek and Latin poetry are quantitative, a pattern of long and short syllables; English meters are primarily accentual. I am unconvinced of the wisdom of attempting to substitute stressed syllables for long, unstressed for short, as a means of suggesting the original rhythm, particularly in the case of the lyric meters Horace is using. The attempts I have seen result in poems that I cannot read with ease and pleasure. A rhythm that can convey without irritation as much of the total poem as possible to readers accustomed to English meters is required.

[2] *Roman Imperial Civilisation* (New York, 1959), pp. xv, 315.

[3] Some indication of these meters will be found in the Introduction to Books I–III, but I have not thought it necessary to attempt a detailed exposition of them.

My own course is unlikely to please everyone, or perhaps anyone. Some of the lyrics I have translated in a comparatively free rhythm, but I found that I needed a set pattern in which to work. For many of the poems I have employed syllabic meters that match the numbers of syllables in the original lines. This gives one point of correspondence with the Latin meters, but I am not pretending that it can bring the effect of those meters into English; it gives the desirable quality of alienness without, I hope, awkwardness; and it allows some freedom in placing the stresses, together with a basic control of the rhythmic pattern. I have tried as often as possible to follow the original in such matters as run-on and end-stopped lines and stanzas.

Horace calls himself "a painstaking minor poet, shaping my lyrics" (iv. 2). Nowhere does he take more pains than with word-order, and nowhere is he more baffling to the English translator. He is free of those "fussy little words that blur our uninflected English," and his lyrics "can give the impression of being built up of clean-cut blocks of stone."[4] He intensifies by at times powerful, at times witty, word-order: antithetic adjectives succeed each other, though they modify antithetic nouns, which are also placed together; adjective and noun are kept apart in order to embrace the entire activity of the remainder of the sentence or clause; details gradually and teasingly reveal themselves before the total picture is before us. There are times when the nature of the language is stretched to the utmost, as in the third stanza of iii. 4, where the adjective *fabulosae* ("legendary") is separated from its noun *palumbes* ("doves") by almost the entire stanza. A

---

[4] L. P. Wilkinson, *Horace and His Lyric Poetry* (Cambridge, 1951), pp. 145, 156.

simpler example of Horace's way of ordering words may be seen in the opening of i. 31, "Quid dedicatum poscit Apollinem," where the verb of praying comes between the adjective indicating the recent consecration of a shrine and the noun naming the god: the word-order may be said to put the prayer in the shrine. The translator has two courses: to experiment with some of the techniques of e. e. cummings, or to content himself with the few moments when English allows him to match the Latin effect and regretfully let the rest go. I have been tempted by the former but have taken the latter course.

To sacrifice effects gained in the original by rhythm and word-order means a considerable loss. Does enough remain to justify translating at all? Granted the importance of every detail of a poem's structure, it is possible to say that enough remains if one can preserve the situation, the basic structure of thought and feeling, the tone, and the imagery, and can employ word-order, rhythm, and music so that the former elements are strongly and lucidly conveyed. If this translation enables the reader to grasp and enjoy, for example, the skill with which Horace moves, by an easy process of association, from a snowy mountain to a girl in a corner in i. 9, and from an outburst of joy through vehement hatred to reluctant admiration in i. 37, then it will be of some use.

I have tried to make in each case a poem that can be read with pleasure by itself and that is accurate, with the provisions already stated, to its original. I have used the word-order and diction of ordinary American speech as a basis, departing from it where a special heightening was demanded. The result is less "artificial," more colloquial, than the original in many instances, but I have tried to avoid vulgarizing and have used a fully colloquial style only in poems whose tone permitted it. I have occasionally taken the liberty of generalizing an image where Horace's particularity would be excessively puzzling for the common reader (as in i. 28. 2), of clarifying allusions in the translation itself rather than in the notes, and of using more familiar names for deities than the original. The freest translation is ii. 11, which generalizes particulars in a carefree way and condenses six to five stanzas: this was one of my earliest attempts; I should not do it this way if I were starting over again, but my attempts at revision have all been weaker poetically, and I prefer to let it stand. I have tried to keep some of the music of alliteration, assonance, and internal rhyme of the originals, but as a general feature of style, not by matching effect for effect.

I have said that I wanted to make English poems that can be read with pleasure; in Dryden's words, "a passable beauty when the original Muse is absent." But I believe a translation should be good, but not too good; it should leave a reader with the sense that more, much more, can be found in the original work. This goal, at least, I am sure to have achieved.

The Latin text used is that edited by C. E. Bennett for the "Loeb Classical Library." I have sometimes, where it seemed warranted, followed the variant readings in this edition, and I have translated i. 28 as a single poem. In both translation and annotation I am heavily indebted to the commentaries in *Horace: Odes and Epodes* (Boston, 1934), edited by C. E. Bennett and revised by John C. Rolfe.

The most stimulating introductions to Horatian lyric are the small book by L. P. Wilkinson, *Horace and His Lyric Poetry* (Cambridge, 1951), and the essay by C. M. Bowra in *Inspiration and Poetry* (London, 1955). Excellent and very thorough criticism of many of the poems is contained in Eduard Fraenkel's *Horace* (Oxford, 1957). W. Y. Sellar's *Horace and the Elegiac Poets* (Oxford, 1891) gives a sound general treatment of the poet's life and works and provides a Victorian viewpoint that contrasts strikingly with Wilkinson's. Gilbert Highet's *Poets in a Landscape* (New York, 1957) has some good analyses and places the poet in the countryside of which he wrote. In his *Translating Horace* (Oxford, 1956), J. B. Leishman offers an approach to the problems and thirty translations, both of which differ radically from the present book.

A Handbook of Latin Literature (London, 1936), by H. J. Rose, and Moses Hadas' *A History of Latin Literature* (New York, 1952) are good introductions to the literary background of the poems. *Methuen's History of the Greek and Roman World* provides a basic historical background in Volumes V and VI, by Frank Burr Marsh and Edward T. Salmon, respectively. Harold Mattingly's *Roman Imperial Civilisation* (New York, 1959) is a helpful exposition of various aspects of its subject—geographical, social, philosophical. The opening chapters of Charles Cochrane's *Christianity and Classical Culture* (Oxford, 1940) offer a good sketch of Augustan ideals and achievements.

I am grateful to my former teacher, the Reverend William Quilty, S.J., who made me see in Horace not a dead language but a live poet. For their early and continued encouragement, I wish to thank in particular Mme H. M. de Thierry, Dr. Donald Connors, Mr. and Mrs. Robert Hazel, and Dr. Paul Memmo. For her patience, assistance, and willingness to live on Horatian terms, "longing for just enough," I owe my greatest debt to my wife.

ODES

INTRODUCTION TO BOOKS ONE, TWO, AND THREE

In collecting the eighty-eight lyrics on which he had labored intensively for almost a decade, Horace saw them as a total body of work and arranged them accordingly. The first book opens with a poem declaring his devotion to Maecenas and his pride in his vocation; the third book closes with a poem in the same meter announcing unequivocally the quality of his achievement. The intervening lyrics are placed with the same painstaking care that Horace shows in ordering the words of a single poem. It is hardly possible. of course, to arrange such a collection so that each poem occupies an inevitable place, and the reader need have no qualms about random sampling; but the order of the poems is such that it strengthens each book and the collection as a whole by its grouping of poems on related themes, its juxtaposition of contrasting subjects and moods, and its use of recurrent themes. I will note just a few examples, most of them in Book I, and leave to the reader the pleasure of discovering others for himself.

Most striking of all is the way Horace employs the first nine lyrics of the first book to demonstrate his thematic variety and his metrical virtuosity. The first poem has already been noted: after a vivid sketch of the varieties of human pursuits and pleasures, Horace declares his dedication to poetry. The meter in the First Asclepiadean: - - - ∪ ∪ - ‖ - ∪ ∪ - ∪ ◡ The second poem is a cry for a redeemer from the terrors of civil war and ends by seeing Augustus in that role. It is in the Sapphic strophe: - ∪ - - - ‖ ∪ ∪ - ∪ - ◡ (3 times); - ∪ ∪ - ◡ . A propempticon, wishes for a favorable voyage, that testifies to Horace's affection for Vergil begins the third lyric, which then turns to a meditation on human courage, ambition, and folly. The stanza is a frequent one in the lyrics, quatrains consisting of two Second Asclepiadean couplets: – – – ◡ ◡ – ◡ ◡ ; – – – ◡ ◡ – ‖ – ◡ ◡ – ◡ ◡̆ .

With the fourth lyric we are into a typically Horatian celebration of spring that leads to the shadow of death and its contrast with present pleasures. For the only time in the lyrics Horace uses a quatrain made up of two Fourth Archilochian strophes: – ◡ ◡ – ◡ ◡ – ‖ ◡ ◡ – ◡ ◡ – ◡ – ◡ – ◡ ; ◡ – ◡ – ◡ ‖ – ◡ – ◡ – ◡ . The length of the first line poses a problem to the translator; English lyrics seldom use seven-foot, eighteen-syllable lines. The fifth lyric is one of Horace's most delicate and witty, a seemingly objective comment on a fickle young lady that ends by revealing that the speaker is one of her victims. The meter is the Fourth Asclepiadean: – – – ◡ ◡ – ‖ – ◡ ◡ – ◡ ◡̆ (twice); – – – ◡ ◡ – ◡̆ ; – – – ◡ ◡ – ◡ ◡̆ . My version is guilty of an excessive shortening of the first two lines of each quatrain, but an attempt to rectify this produced a weaker, padded poem.

In the sixth lyric, Horace modestly, amusingly, but firmly refuses a suggestion, probably by Maecenas or Augustus, that he write heroic poems and insists that he is a light versifier. He employs the Third Asclepiadean quatrain: – – – ◡ ◡ – ‖ – ◡ ◡ – ◡ ◡̆ (3 times); – – – ◡ ◡ – ◡̆ ◡̆ . The seventh lyric celebrates the countryside about Tibur but shades off into a praise of wine: the connection is made by means of Plancus' implied longing for his home. Horace uses two Alcmanic strophes for each quatrain, dactyllic hexameters followed by dactyllic tetrameters. Lydia is rebuked in the eighth lyric for unmanning Sybaris, in a meter Horace never uses again, quatrains made of two Second Sapphic strophes: –◡◡–◡–◡̱; –◡–––‖◡◡––◡◡–◡–◡̱. The ninth lyric is a variation upon a poem by Alcaeus, appropriately in the Alcaic strophe: ◡̱–◡––‖–◡◡–◡◡ (twice); ◡̱–◡–––◡–◡; –◡◡–◡◡–◡–◡̱.

These first nine lyrics are thus a tour de force, a statement of themes, and a bold declaration of Horace's intention to achieve in Latin what had been accomplished by the lyric poets of Greece. Sappho and Alcaeus, the sixth-century poets of Lesbos, were his particular masters, and the Sapphic and Alcaic strophes were his favorite meters, but he draws on the whole tradition of Greek lyric.

Horace frequently places poems for complementary effects. So i. 30, the brief invocation of Venus at a private shrine, is followed by a longer prayer to Apollo at a public temple; the "conversion" poem, i. 34, ending with a comment on Fortune, is immediately followed by the solemn address to Fortuna in 35. But Horace just as frequently seeks the effect of contrast. After the celebration of Augustus in i. 12, we have a poem in contrasting tone and meter on jealousy; the grave lament for Quintilius, i. 24, is preceded by the charming wooing of Chloe and followed by a scornful comment on an aging beauty; the powerful, complex lyric of triumph, i. 37, is juxtaposed to the neatness and brevity of i. 38, which quietly concludes Book I.

It was natural enough for Horace to separate poems with very similar subjects and themes. His disposition of the lyrics gives, however, the effect of the appearance, disappearance, and return of motifs: civil peace and disorder, the value of poetry, the brevity of life, the pleasures of wine, the pains and joys of love, and the delights of a country life. It is worth noting, at least, that in Book I the theme of Augustus and civil peace is the focus of 2, 12 and 37, and, in contrast, that Lydia makes her first appearance in a poem of seemingly disinterested rebuke, 8, next in a poem of explicit jealousy, 13, and finally in the triumphantly contemptuous 25.

One group of lyrics has traditionally been singled out for special comment. Horace opens the third book with six poems that have earned the label of "Roman Odes." They are, clearly enough, "bound together by their common meter, their solemn style, by the fact that none of them is addressed to an individual, by the affinity of their main themes, and by the central position which Augustus and his rule occupy in them."[1] The opening of iii. 1, with its deliberate assumption of the role of priest, is enough to tell us that Horace has forsaken for the time being the role of light versifier he so frequently assumes. But the six poems have sometimes tempted critics into the presumption that all were written at the same time and according to a deliberate sequence, which seems very doubtful. Their sequence as it now stands is surely deliberate; but this was decided, it is safer to guess, after the composition of the poems, and there is nothing rigidly mechanical about the relationships of the six. Their concerns are with the private and public virtues and vices that can preserve or destroy Rome, and in this they are linked to Augustus' program of moral reform. The most difficult of these poems are 3 and 4. Wilkinson's interpretation of the former as a kind of parable in which Troy symbolizes "the decadent Republic" is worth considering;[2] Fraenkel sees the latter centered on the power of the Muses, "as champions of order and peace against the forces of violence and destruction."[3]

1 Eduard Fraenkel, *Horace* (Oxford, 1957), p. 260.

2 *Horace and His Lyric Poetry*, p. 73.

3 *Horace*, p. 281.

16

This group of "political lyrics" has received excessive praise and equally excessive scorn, not always for its literary merits. Horace reminds himself as well as us that his lyrics have other concerns, in the closing stanza of iii. 3 and the grace and wit and playfulness of iii. 7. He can be both "priest of the Muses" and "poet of parties," and it is dangerous to overemphasize either role.

I wish to explore more fully several of the characteristics of Horatian lyric noted in the General Introduction. It should be remembered, however, that generalization about the practice of a lyric poet is never easy and is frequently unprofitable, and that what matters is less the general practice than the particular means by which a single poem realizes itself.

It is possible to make a broad distinction between two modes of structure in Horatian lyric. I shall take the liberty of calling them "formal" and "casual." While I shall discuss them separately, I do not mean to suggest that the two modes do not at times blend in a single poem.

A good, small example of the formally constructed lyric is i. 9. It begins with the invocation of the god who is its subject and a listing of his attributes in the first two stanzas. The final attribute, Mercury's love of a trick, leads naturally into the next two stanzas, the first dealing with a comic trick, the second with a trick that aids the tragic figure of Priam. The last stanza springs naturally from Mercury's role as escort to the living and develops his function as escort to the dead, rounding out the tribute to the god by seeing him at home in two worlds. Neatness and balance are achieved by the grouping of the stanzas. This mode of structure may be seen more elaborately in i. 12; it occurs frequently when the poet is engaged in public celebration of a god or hero, but it is also used in poems of private occasions. It may be ventured that this structure is closely related to the tradition of sung lyric, whereas the second mode of structure seems logically to come from the circumstances of lyric spoken or read.

The term "casual" for this second mode is arbitrary and may be misleading. I do not mean to suggest that Horace, one of the most technically scrupulous of all poets, is careless. This structural mode is based on association; it is deliberately cultivated and may owe something to Horace's practice in the *Satires*. It is a structure familiar to the reader of Donne and Marvell, occurring more often in their work than in Jonson's or Herrick's, the English poets with whom Horace is usually linked.

Integer vitae scelerisque purus begins i. 12, and it would seem we are to get a moral lyric on integrity. This impression is sustained through the first two stanzas, though we may begin to suspect the hyperbolic quality of the geographical allusions. The next two stanzas keep a perfectly straight face, but we cannot, as the poet advances his proof of the power of rectitude and insists on the size of that wolf. We are then launched into a further series of hyperbolic geographical allusions in the last two stanzas, all leading to the avowal of love. And so the poem that began with *integer vitae* ends with *dulce loquentem:* we have moved from a man's righteousness to a girl's chatter.

This is the structure characteristic of many of Horace's finest and best-known lyrics. I have noted i. 9 and i. 37 in the General Introduction and will call attention to just a few others: ii. 8 moves from Horace's narrow escape from a falling tree to the power of Alcaeus' songs; iii. 4 hails the return of

Augustus as it opens and comments wistfully on the poet's graying hair and calmer temper as it closes; the spring sacrifice to Faunus in the third stanza of i. 4 calls up the knocking of death at human doors in the opening of the fourth. Our awareness of this mode of structure can clarify many of the lyrics (though i. 7 is, to my mind, an unsuccessful use of it), and this is especially true of some of Horace's final stanzas. The finale of ii. 14, for example, points up, not the theme of death to which we have been attending, but the other side of the coin, the folly of hoarding the good things of life until we cannot enjoy them.

This "casual" technique can be effective on a smaller scale. The departure of Regulus in iii. 5 is superbly managed, and the simile of the last stanza comes somewhat unexpectedly but with the *curiosa felicitas*, the rightness that comes of taking pains, that Petronius found characteristic of Horace. The crowning touch, however, is in the last line, as Horace gives to the resort of Tarentum a "casual" epithet, *Lacedaemonium*, "founded by Spartans."

One sign of technical mastery in a poet who writes in a time when lyric is more often spoken than sung is his management of the line, couplet, and stanza. When lyric is spoken or read, the poet can gain power and subtlety of effect by playing the thought-units of the poem against the metrical units, stopping the sentence in mid-line, or running the thought on from one stanza to the next. It is, of course, a dangerous freedom; the unskilled poet can lose the advantages of control that the metrical units provide without gaining any compensation.

Horace's early lyrics, the *Epodes*, work most often with the couplet as the thought-unit as well as the metrical unit. In the *carmina*, the metrical unit is the quatrain, even when this is

built of two couplets; and Horace is equally adept at using the
metrical unit for controlling and pointing up the thought and
at counterpointing the two units. The former technique will be
evident enough, even in translation; the latter requires at least
one example. Here is the fourth stanza and the opening of the
fifth in i. 9:

> quid sit futurum cras, fuge quaerere et
> quem Fors dierum cumque dabit, lucro
>   appone nec dulces amores
>   sperne puer neque tu choreas,
>
> donec virenti canities abest
> morosa.

It should be evident that the poet is counterpointing his
units of meter and thought with great dexterity. Some advan-
tage is taken of the first couplet to balance "what tomorrow
may hold" and "however many days Fortune may grant," of
the second line to sum up the clause as the line ends with the
one word *lucro* ("as gain"); but the verbs *fuge* and *appone*
are not balanced in the couplet: *appone* is pointed up by its
position in the sentence and by running on the second line, as
sperne is by running on the third line, which then gives us a
sudden balance between *appone* and *sperne*. And the sentence
is not completed until we have the vision of old age in the first
line of the next stanza, which itself is not completed until we
run the line on to complete the sentence by the isolated and
emphasized *morosa*.

With this passage before us, we may note briefly some other
aspects of Horace's art. Some of the skill of his word-order is
already evident; let me point also to the effective juxtaposition
of *dabit* and *lucro*, to the placing of *puer* ("while you are

young") immediately after *sperne* ("despise") and of both these key words within the activities that are not to be rejected, *dulces amores* and *choreas,* and to the powerful contrast of growth and decay achieved by following *virenti* with *canities.* There is, too, the Horatian music that binds the Horatian sense: the delicate intertwining alliterations of *f, c,* and *d,* the assonance on *e,* the internal rhyming of *Fors, amores,* and *choreas,* of *sperne* and *puer.*

This brief analysis has shown the "mosaic of words, in which every word by sound, by position, and by meaning, diffuses its influence to right and left and over the whole; the minimum in compass and number of symbols, the maximum achieved in the effectiveness of those symbols, all that is Roman, and . . . of excellence unsurpassed."[4] This is the despair of an English translator, and I shall not discourage the reader and myself with further examples.

No lyric poet can hope to encompass the entire range of human experience. There are regions Horace cannot and does not enter. For the expression of the full intensity of love for another human being we go to Sappho or Catullus or Donne, of religious awe and anguish and yearning to Fray Luis de Leon or John of the Cross, Herbert or Hopkins. There are times, though, when Horace will surprise us, as in iii. 25: the Apollonian poet can recognize in himself as well as others Dionysian forces.

It is in the "middle range" of human experience that Horace is supreme, and his limitations are, perhaps, one reason for his continued popularity. We have all felt what Horace feels far more often than what Catullus or Hopkins feels,

---

4 Nietzsche, quoted in Wilkinson, *Horace and His Lyric Poetry,* p. 4.

whether this is to our credit or not. As J. W. Mackail says, "the cardinal matter was to strike in the centre."[5] Of a relatively ordinary life[6]—ordinary even in that he felt, as we now feel, great political forces in motion that threatened his settled way of living—he fashioned magnificent poetry: common experience found itself voiced with uncommon art.

[5] *Latin Literature* (New York, 1895), p. 113.

[6] What may strike a modern reader as anything but ordinary, the sexual relationships with boys as well as women, was in fact normal Roman behavior, as may be noted by the tone of the lyrics, a tone that cannot be easily duplicated in modern writing, where defiance, revulsion, or a sense of guilt are inevitable in dealing with such experience.

BOOK ONE

I · 1

Maecenas, descendant of a royal family,
O my rock of refuge and dear source of honor:
there are men who delight in gathering dust
on Olympic chariots; when their blazing wheels
clear the turn, and the palm crowns them, they are
lords of the earth, lofted among the gods;
one man's joy is to hold the highest office
bestowed by the public whim of the Romans;
another's, to know his barns are stuffed with all
the grain from all the threshing floors of Africa.
No treasures could talk the man who happily
breaks hard clods with his hoe on the family farm
into plowing the Myrtoan, a shivering sailor.
The trader, scared by roughhousing winds and waves,
sings in praise of the peaceful country town
where he was born; soon he refits his ships,
a lower standard of living is not for him.
There's a man not above a cup of good wine
and a pause in the day's occupation, sometimes beneath
the blossoming arbutus, sometimes by a quiet stream.
Many thrill to the soldiers' life, the camp,
the sound of horn and trumpet, the battles so hated
by mothers. Under a cold night sky the hunter
stays, not a thought for his sweet young wife,
if the sure hounds have sighted a deer, or if

a boar of the hills bursts through his finest nets.
As for me, the prize for poets, the crown
of ivy, makes me one with the gods; in shady
woods, among the light-stepping nymphs and satyrs,
I am far from the crowd, while Euterpe allows me
her flute, and Polyhymnia does not refuse
to tune for me the lyre of Lesbos.
And should you rank my songs with the masters',
I shall walk tall, my head will touch stars.

More than enough, the omens of snow and sleet
sent by the Father to earth: his right hand glowed
as he hurled his bolts at our sacred hills: the city
        trembled with terror,

the people trembled, fearing the return of the Flood,
the days when Pyrrha wailed of weird happenings,
when Proteus drove his whole seal herd to roam
        high on the mountains,

all the fish flocked close to the tops of the elms,
places where the doves had always rested,
and the frightened deer swam through the highest
        stretches of ocean.

We saw the yellow Tiber, waves driven
raging back from his Etruscan bank,
charge to batter the royal monument and the
        temple of Vesta,

the rivergod overplaying the part of
avenger of Ilia's wrongs, rising, without
Jove's permission, far beyond the left bank,
        too fond a husband.

They will hear that citizens honed for each other
their swords, better used killing Parthians,
and fought: the children—they are few: blame the parents—
        will
                hear of the fighting.

To what god shall our people cry: "Prevent
the fall of the empire"? How shall the holy virgins
beg Vesta's intercession, who closes her
    ears to their chanting?

Who is Jove's choice for the role of redeemer
from sin? Come to us at last, we pray,
a cloud as a mantle on your shining shoulder,
    prophet Apollo;

or come, if you would rather, smiling Venus
of Eryx, Joy and Longing hovering by you;
or Mars, our founder, look on this abandoned
    nation, your children:

O the game has gone on too long, you have had
your fill, your pleasures of shining helmets and war cries,
the hard face of the Marsian soldier meeting a
    blood-soaked opponent.

Or Mercury, wing-footed son of Maia,
come to earth, changing the shape of a god
to the shape of a man, pleased to be called by us
    Caesar's avenger:

may you long delay your return to heaven, long
may you love to stay with the people of Romulus,
may you never be shocked by our sins, may no wind
    suddenly snatch you

away from us; here may you glory in triumphs,
here rejoice to be called "father" and "first one,"
leave no Parthian raiders unpunished, while you are
    leading us, Caesar.

May Venus, Cyprian goddess,
    may the bright constellation, Helen's twin brothers,
and the father of winds, keeping
    all but northwestern breezes under lock and key,

watch over you, ship that holds our
    Vergil in trust: may you deposit him safely
on the shores of Greece, as I pray,
    and preserve the man who is half my very soul.

Oak and three layers of bronze made
    his breastplate, whoever he was who first ventured
a thin ship out on rough waters,
    with no fear of the rowdy Southwester's struggles

with the blasting wind from the north,
    no fear of stars that mean rain, or the mad Southwind,
sole lord of the Adriatic,
    at whose whim the waters rise high or grow calmer.

What could he fear in death's footstep,
    a man who had seen with dry eyes the sea monsters,
seen the sea at its stormiest,
    the notorious cliffs on the coast of Epirus?

In vain God in his wisdom planned
    to divide the land by the sea's separations,
if, for all that, ungodly ships
    are crossing the waters that he placed out of bounds.

The human race is ready for
    anything: it rushes into forbidden ways.

Prometheus, a ready one,
    clever and wicked, descended with fire for men.

Once fire was stolen from heaven,
    sickness that wasted the flesh and a newborn swarm
of fevers spread over the earth,
    and death, that must come, that before had been lagging

far behind, then stepped up its pace.
    Daedalus tested the empty air with his wings:
no god ever gave them to men;
    Hercules pushed his way through the entrance to Hell.

There is no climb too high for men;
    we are stupid enough to try to reach heaven,
and Jove gets no rest from our sins,
    can never put aside his lightning and thunder.

Winter's fists unclench at the touch of spring and western
   breezes,
      dried-out keels are drawn down to the waves,
flocks are no longer at ease in stables, farmers at firesides,
      meadows are no longer white with frost.

Under a hovering moon come dancers led by white Aphrodite,
      the slender Graces join hands with the nymphs
lightly to waltz on the grass, as Cyclops under sweltering
   Vulcan
      forge bolts of lightning for the storms to come.

Now is the time to garland glistening hair with green myrtle
      or flowers, as the freed earth rejoices in birth;
now a gift to Faunus is proper, in shadowy groves a victim,
      whatever is to his taste, ewe lamb or kid.

Death with his drained-out face will drum at destitute cottage
      and royal castle. You have been lucky, Sestius:
all of life is only a little, no long-term plans are allowed.
      Soon night and half-remembered shapes and drab

Pluto's walls will be closing in; enter his halls and you're
   done with
      tosses of dice that crown you toastmaster,
marveling glances at slim young Lycidas, for whom all the
   boys are
      now burning, and the girls will soon catch fire.

What slim and sweetly scented boy
presses you to the roses, Pyrrha,
    in your favorite grotto?
        For whom is your blond hair styled,

deceptively simple? Ah, how often he'll sob
over your faithless conversions, staring
    stupidly at the black
        winds and wild seas. He has you

now, for him you have a golden glow,
ever contented, ever loving
    he hopes, unaware of the
        tricky breeze. Poor things, for whom

you glitter before you're tried. The temple
wall with its plaque serves notice: I
    have hung my wet clothes up
        and bowed to the sea god's power.

I · 6

Varius, a poet highflying as Homer, will write
you up, your courage, your conquest of our enemy,
the deeds by land and sea of daring soldiers
        with you as their general.

As for me, Agrippa, to tell of these things,
or the dread peeve of Achilles, who never knew
how to give in, or clever Ulysses' sea voyage,
        or the cruel house of Atreus,

I do not try: major themes, minor poet;
propriety and the non-belligerent Muse
forbid me to spoil Caesar's praises and yours
        with a botched-up job.

What poet is worthy to write of Mars in his armor
of adamant, or Meriones, blackened
with Trojan dust, or Diomed, aided by Athena,
        in whom gods met their match?

I am a poet of parties, battles of virgins
valiantly fighting off boys with their manicured nails
I celebrate, my heart at ease or on fire,
        in my usual featherbrained way.

Others may sing the praises of Rhodes or Mitylene,
    Ephesus, or the walls of Corinth that face
two seas, Thebes that is famous for Bacchus, Apollo's own
    Delphi,
        or the valley of Tempe in Thessaly.

There are some who have only one job, to praise Athena's
    city with songs that go on forever,
and to search all sources for leaves for their olive crowns.
        There are many to honor Juno,

singing of Argos, breeder of horses, and golden Mycenae.
    But for me, neither sturdy Lacedaemon
nor the generous fields of Larisa impress me as much
        as the Sibyl's echoing grotto,

Anio's leaping torrent, the grove of Tiburnus, the orchards
    watered by the running brooks.
Wind from the south often clears the sky as it chases
        dark clouds away; it does not always

bring showers: keep this in mind, Plancus, call a halt
    to the burdens and sorrows of life
with a cup of good wine, wherever you are, under
        bright banners in camp or at home

in the deep shades of Tibur. Teucer was exiled from Salamis
    by his father, yet they say that he drank
till his forehead was ruddy with wine, put on garlands of
        poplar, and said to his sorrowful friends:

"Fortune is kinder than father: friends and companions,
    let us go wherever it takes us.
Do not give up while Teucer commands and protects you.
    For Apollo is faithful: he promised

a new country would see a second Salamis.
    Heroes, you and I have often
come through worse times: today, banish worry with wine;
    back to the deep sea tomorrow."

Tell me, Lydia, in the name
 of all that's holy, why are you set on wrecking Sybaris
with loving? Why does he loathe
  the sunlit field? Dirt and sweat never bothered him
   before.

Why won't he join his fellow
 soldiers at cavalry practice, or curb his Gallic stallion
with a jagged bit in its mouth?
  Why is he scared of a splash in yellow Tiber? Why does he

avoid the rubbing oil
 as if it were the blood of a viper? Why doesn't he show
  off now
all the bruises on his arms?
  And to think he once threw for the record with discus
   and javelin!

Why does he lie low, like the
 son of seaborn Thetis before the fall of Troy with all
its bitter tears, afraid that
  Trojan troops and death would come of wearing the
   clothes of a man?

See, the snows on Mount Soracte glare against
the sky, and the branches strain, giving way
    beneath the weight, and the fluent
        waters stand fast, fixed by the bitter freeze.

Take the chill off, piling plenty of logs
by the fireside, and pour out the wine, four years
    aging, from the Sabine jar,
        Thaliarchus, with a free hand.

Leave the rest to the gods, for once they quiet
the winds that are warring with the roaring
    sea, cypress and ancient
        ashtree are troubled no longer.

Do not ask of tomorrow what it may hold;
mark in the black each day you are granted
    by Chance: you are young, no
        sneering at loving and dancing

while the sap rises and whining old age
stays away. Now is the time for playing field
    and public squares with soft
        whispers as night covers lovers meeting,

and now is the time for giveaway giggles
from the far corner and the girl in hiding,
    and the prize snatched from her
        arm or finger that (almost) resists.

Mercury, smooth-talking grandson of Atlas,
giver of language, founder of graceful games,
clever sculptor of the crude behavior
    of primitive man,

my song is of you, messenger of great Jove
and all the gods, creator of the curved lyre,
cunning, getting away with what suits you
    by playing a trick.

Once, you were just a boy, when Apollo tried
to browbeat you into giving back cows
you had lifted, he found himself minus his
    quiver, and he laughed.

And you were the guide when Priam brought ransom
from Ilium: the proud sons of Atreus,
the Myrmidon watchfires, the Troy-hating camp
    never noticed him.

You escort deserving souls to their happy
places, with a golden staff shepherd the crowd
of shades: you are at home with the gods above
    and the gods below.

Don't ask, Leuconoë, the forbidden question, how long
the gods have given to you and to me: don't imagine
fortunetellers know. Better to take what is coming,
whether Jove allows us more winters, or this that now
wearies the Etruscan sea as it beats on the cliffs
is the last. Be sensible: strain the wine: in a little life,
take no long looks ahead. As we talk, time spites us
and runs: reap today: save no hopes for tomorrow.

Whose praises will you sing, Clio, to the lyre
or the clear-voiced flute? Is he man or hero?
Is he a god? Whose name will echo toy with
    over and over

along the shady slopes of Mount Helicon,
on the peak of Pindus or chilly Haemus,
the mountain whose trees were entranced and followed
    Orpheus' singing,

who knew his mother's art so well he could hold
the currents of rushing waters and swift winds,
and charm the oaks until they heard and followed
    his sweet-sounding lyre?

What should come first in my song but the honor
due to the Father, ruler of men and gods,
whose realm is the earth and the sea and the sky
    in all its seasons?

From him comes forth nothing that surpasses him,
and nothing lives that is like him or near him.
But the place that is nearest his in honor
    is that of Pallas,

mighty in battle; my song will not forget
Bacchus, and the virgin Diana, death to
ravaging beasts, and you, Phoebus, feared for your
    accurate arrows.

And I sing of Hercules, and Leda's sons,
one a famous master of horses and one
of his fists: when their bright constellation shines
    over the sailors,

the stirred-up waters stream down from the cliffside,
the winds die down, and the clouds hurry away,
and the towering wave, at their command, lies
    at ease on the sea.

After these shall I sing first of Romulus,
or the quiet times when Pompilius ruled,
or the splendid reign of Tarquin, or Cato
    and his noble death?

I shall show my thanks in a song to honor
Regulus, and men like Scaurus and Paulus,
who gave up his life when Hannibal conquered,
    and Fabricius.

He and Camillus and Curius, whose hair
was untrimmed, these were men trained by poverty
for warfare and life on the family land
    in a small farmhouse.

Like a tree that grows as time slips by, this is
the fame of Marcellus: the Julian star
shines in the midst of all others like the moon
    among smaller lights.

Father and guardian of the human race,
son of Saturn, destiny has given you
charge of great Caesar: may you rule over all;
    and under you, Caesar.

Whether he leads in triumphal procession
the conquered Parthians, threats to Latium,
or Seres and Indians from the Eastern
    lands on our border,

under you his justice will rule the wide earth:
you shake Olympus with your great chariot;
you strike groves made unclean by filthy doings
    with angry lightning.

Lydia, when you rave about
    Telephus and his rose-pink neck, Telephus and
his wax-smooth arms, ah god, but my
    liver is burning and swelling up with black bile.

Then my mind and my complexion
    slip from their moorings, and a teardrop secretly
slides down my cheek, a certain proof
    that my inwards are being eaten by steady fires.

This fevers me: when your snowy
    shoulders show bruises from squabbles after too much
wine, or that headstrong boy has made
    an indelible mark with his teeth on your lips.

No, if you would listen to me,
    you would never hope that he would be true, a crude
crusher of lips that were sweetened
    by Venus with her own quintessence of nectar.

They are happy, three times over,
    who are held by a tie that remains unbroken,
whose love no bitter words divide,
    and who never are parted before their last day.

I · 14

O ship, waves are rising once more to carry you
out to sea. O, guard yourself. Try your hardest to
    reach the harbor. Don't you see
        how the sides are stripped of their oars,

how the shattered mainmast and the yardarms groan in
the gale from Africa, how no cincture of ropes
    supports the hull, which scarcely
        can withstand such tyrannical

waters? You have not a sail still whole, and no gods
left on board to listen when new dangers threaten.
    Much good it does you that pine
        from Pontus made you, that famous

forests fathered you: you brag of your name and class,
but a scared sailor puts little trust in painted
    poops. If you are not doomed to
        be the winds' plaything, be careful.

A while back, I was tired of worry about you:
now I long for you, and I am deeply troubled.
    Steer clear of the seas that rush
        between the gleaming Cyclades.

As Paris, the shepherd who could not be trusted
with his host's wife, carried Helen over the seas,
Nereus held the swift winds in unnatural
    stillness, while he foretold their hard

fate: "The omens are evil; you bring home a bride
the Greeks will come after with many a soldier,
for they will take oaths to destroy your marriage and
    the ancient kingdom of Priam.

O how the horses and the soldiers will be drenched
with sweat! You are bringing great grief to the people
of Troy! Even now Pallas readies her helmet,
    her shield and chariot and rage.

It will do you no good to trust Venus so much
that you pretty up your hair, and sing, to a peace-
loving lyre, songs that are fit for a woman's taste;
    no good to hide in your bedroom

from the heavy spears and the Cretan arrows and
the clangor of battle and the swift pursuit of
Ajax: for all this, though too late, you will dirty
    adulterous hair in the dust.

Are you unconcerned by Laertes' son Ulysses,
death to your people, or by Nestor of Pylos?
Fearless Teucer of Salamis is after you,
    Sthenelus is on you, who knows

how to fight, and when he must handle the horses
is no mean charioteer. You will learn to know
Meriones. Fierce Diomed, greater than his
    father, rages in search of you,

and you, like a deer with no more thoughts of grazing
once it sees a wolf somewhere else in the valley,
head back and breathing hard and scared stiff you will run,
    whatever you swore to your girl.

The anger of Achilles will postpone the day
of sorrow for Troy and for the Trojan women;
but after the destined number of years, Greek fires
    will burn the homes of the Trojans."

I · 16

Lovelier daughter of a lovely mother,
my libelous lines are at your disposal:
      get rid of them as you please, burn them,
          or consign them to the Adriatic.

Not Cybele, not the dweller who shudders
the priestess' soul in the Pythian sanctum,
      not Bacchus, not the wild priests clashing
          their clanging cymbals, none of these shakes us

like bitter anger: nothing can stop it, not
hard Noric swords nor the shipwrecking sea nor
      raging fire nor Jupiter himself
          roaring down upon us in rough weather.

They say that Prometheus made us of mud
and was forced to graft to it pieces of all
      the creatures: he added to our breasts
          the wild fury of a maddened lion.

Anger set the stage for Thyestes' tragic
finale: it has always been the first cause
      of tall cities' obliteration:
          where once were walls an enemy army

impresses the earth with an arrogant plow.
Keep tight rein on your temper: I was a boy,
      an easy mark, a hothead, and so
          I did you wrong when I rushed into verse

like a lunatic; now I look to convert
my verses from bitter to sweet, if only
   (now that I take it all back) we are
      friends once more, and once more your heart is
      mine.

I · 17

Faunus often leaves Mount Lycaeus, quickly
coming to lovely Lucretilis, and while
    he is here, he keeps my goats from the
        heat of the sun and the wind and the rain.

No harm will come to the stinking husband's
harem, as they wander through the safe forest
    after hidden arbutus and thyme,
        and the little kids have no fear of green

serpents, and no fear of Mars' darling the wolf,
my dear Tyndaris, whenever the charming
    panpipes have echoed from the sloping
        valleys and the smooth rocks of Ustica.

The gods watch over me, the gods are fond of
my poems and prayers. Here the fields offer
    their generous harvest, all for you
        the horn will fill to the brim with plenty.

Here is your refuge, in this quiet valley,
from the heat of high summer, and you will sing
    to your lyre of the love for one man
        of Penelope and seagreen Circe;

here you will take no harm, drinking
the wine of Lesbos: Bacchus, that child of rage,
    will not tangle with Mars and set off
        a riot; you will not be afraid of

hotheaded Cyrus (he's not right for you, dear),
his eye always on you, too free with his hands,
    tearing to bits the garland that crowns
        your hair, and your robe that did nothing wrong.

Plant no tree, Varus, before you set the blessed vine
in the fertile soil around Tibur, by Catilus' walls;
for the god gives a hard time to those who are dry
and nothing but wine will chase nagging worry away.
after a cup, who complains of the draft or his income?
Who would not rather praise you, Bacchus, and sweet Venus?
But let no one step off limits with the gifts of Freedom:
be warned by the Centaurs' drunken brawl with the Lapithae,
a fight to the finish, be warned by the god's lack of love for
   Thracians
when wild with desire they can tell right from wrong
by nothing but their lusts. Bright Bassareus, I shall never
arouse your slow anger, nor let daylight violate your
   emblems
all overgrown with leaves. Silence the frenzied drums
and the Berecyntian horn that herald the coming
of Love blind with self, Boasting, empty head held high,
and Trust that can't keep a secret, seen through like glass.

The cruel mother of Cupids,
    and Bacchus, Theban Semele's son, and giddy
Loose-living command me to take
    second thoughts about love, that seemed to be over.

I burn for Glycera's beauty,
    more whitely she glows than the marble of Paros;
I burn with her charming teasing,
    and with the tempting yes-and-no of her glances.

Venus is leaving her Cyprus
    and taking me over entirely, allowing
no songs about Scythians or
    Parthian tricks in flight, nothing not in her field.

Right here, my boys, make me a green
    altar of turf; place the sacred branches right here,
incense, and a bowl of pure wine:
    she comes more kindly when a victim is offered.

Cheap Sabine wine will be your drink, in plain
tankards; from a Greek jar, though, where I stored
and sealed it myself, that day they filled the theater
  with applause for you,

dear lord Maecenas, and the banks of Tiber,
the river of your homeland, and the playful
echo from Mount Vatican answered
  the sounds of your praise.

The best vintages, Caecuban, Calenian,
you may drink when you wish; my goblets hold
no flavor of wine from the vines of Falernus
  or Formia's hills.

Chant the praise of Diana, delicate maidens,
and boys, chant the praises of long-haired Apollo
    and Latona, dearly loved
        by Jupiter, lord of the gods.

Girls, sing of her joy in streams and thick-leaved woodlands,
the cool groves that distinguish Mount Algidus,
    the greenwood of Mount Cragus,
        and Erymanthus' dark forests;

boys, sing as sweet a celebration of Tempe
and of Delos, island where Apollo was born,
    the quiver on his shoulder,
        the lyre that Mercury gave him.

May war with its tears and fearful famine and plague
be lifted from our people and Caesar our lord,
    and visit our enemies,
        if the gods are moved by your prayers.

A clean record and a clear conscience
can do without Moroccan javelins
or bow and quiver stuffed with poisoned arrows,
    my dear Fuscus,

whether one's way is through the blazing sand of
Africa, the unwelcoming heights of Caucasia,
or through the land of legends where the Indus
    pours its waters.

For when I met a wolf in the Sabine woods,
as I was singing the praises of Lalage, walking
far from my farm, not a care in the world,
    unarmed: he ran.

Was he a monster! That soldiering country Apulia
couldn't grow his equal in its broad oak forests,
barren Numidia, nourisher of lions, breeds
    not a bigger.

Put me on a barren plain, where never a tree
renews its leaves in the breezes of summer,
a foggy country where the sky hangs low
    upon the earth;

put me where the chariot of the sun comes
swinging so low that no one can live there:
still will I love my Lalage, her laughter is sweet,
    her chatter charming.

You shy from me, Chloe, like a fawn
seeking on pathless hills its frightened
    mother, scared silly
        by breezes and the big woods.

For if spring's advances make the light
leaves tremble, if green lizards stir
    the bramble bushes, its heart
        knocks and its knees quiver.

Now really, I'm no ferocious tiger
or Moroccan lion, chasing, mauling:
    stop trailing mama now,
        you're ready for a man.

How shall we keep in or limit our grief, so dear
was this man? Teach me a funeral dirge,
Melpomene, gifted by the Father with a clear
    voice and the lyre's music.

So the sleep that lasts forever now covers
Quintilius. Honor, and the sister of Justice,
unbroken Trust, and Truth who walks naked,
    when shall they find his equal?

He dies mourned by many good men,
but by no man more deeply, Vergil, than you.
Useless devotion to beg the gods for Quintilius,
    he was not lent on those terms.

What good would it do to play the lute more sweetly
than Orpheus of Thrace, to whom the trees responded?
Would the blood come back to his thin ghost,
    whom Mercury once and for all

(he does not take kindly to prayers to open the gates)
with his grim staff has gathered to the flock of shades?
It's hard: but patience makes those things lighter
    that we have no power to change.

Less and less often the roaring boys
toss their pebbles against your closed shutters,
they don't rob you of sleep any more, and the
    door hugs its threshold

that once turned gladly all night on its
hinges. You hear fewer and fewer wailing:
"While I spend the long night dying for you, Lydia,
    can you stay sleeping?"

Your turn is coming: a crone alone in the street,
you will cry that your lovers all hate you,
as the Northwind howls like a bacchante
    and the moon is dark,

and the fire of love and longing is in you,
the itch that drives a mare mad for a stallion,
you will rage with the lust that gnaws your belly
    and you will complain

that the goodtime boys now find their fun
with the green ivy and the dark green myrtle,
and the withered leaves are tossed away
    to the winter wind.

I · 26

The Muses love me: let the wild winds carry
my fears and melancholy off to the Cretan
    sea: no matter what Northern king
        threatens us from his cold frontiers,

what fills Tiridates the Parthian with terror,
I am unperturbed. O you who take joy in fresh
    fountains, weave the bright flowers,
        weave them into a garland for Lamia,

sweet Pierian Muse. I can do him no
honor without you: it is fitting that you
    and your sisters, with the lyre of Lesbos,
        with a new style, make him immortal.

Cups are for pleasure: to use them as weapons
is a Thracian trick. Stop behaving like
    savages, and spare Bacchus your brawls
        and bloodshed: he prefers moderation.

When lamps are lit and wine is poured, a Persian
sword is dreadfully out of place: keep it down,
    gentlemen, this shouting's indecent;
        lie quiet and at ease on your couches.

So, you want me to drink up my share of strong
Falernian wine? Only if Megylla's
    brother from Opus tells us what wound,
        what arrow gives him such exquisite pain.

A little reluctant? Either meet my terms
or I don't drink. This passion that's possessed you,
    there's no need for your face to turn red
        over that sort of fire: a freeborn girl

is the kind you go for. Come on, whatever
it is, you can whisper to me.—Ah, poor thing,
    you are into quite a Charybdis,
        you're a boy who deserves a better flame.

What witch or wizard has a Thessalian
charm that can free you? What god has such power?
    You are in three-bodied Chimaera's
        grip: even Pegasus can't get you out.

You were the man who measured the sea and the earth and
    the measureless
        sand, Archytas, and now you are held in
fast, by a puny hillock of paltry dirt, on the seacoast
        near Matinus: what good is it now that you

pried in the airy homes of the gods and let your mind run
        through the turning heavens, as death waited.
Dead is the father of Pelops, who once was the guest of the
    gods;
        so is Tithonus they brought into heaven, and

Minos, who shared the secrets of Jove, and the lower world
        holds Pythagoras on his second trip,
who had once been, he said, the son of Panthous, and took his
        shield from the temple to show that he knew

Trojan times, and that death had seized mere muscles and
    skin:
        he was never, to your mind, a bad judge of
nature and truth. But a single night is waiting for all, and the
        walk on the road of death must come.

Some are the gifts of the Furies for bloodthirsty Mars'
    entertainments;
        death to the sailors is the hungry sea:
old and young makes no difference, funeral crowded on
    funeral,
        cruel Proserpina spares not a head.

I am another victim: the Southwind, that rages when Orion is
    setting, drowned me in Illyrian waves.
Sailor, do not be unkind, refusing to my unburied
    head and bones the gift of a little

shifting sand: and for this, whatever the danger when the
    Eastwind
        hangs over Adriatic waters, may you be
safe, as the woods of Venusia bend in the storm, and may
    riches
        shower on you from their proper sources, the

justice of Jove and of Neptune, keeper of holy Tarentum.
    Do you think it so little, a wrong done
that may later bring harm to your innocent children? And
    maybe the
        need for burial and the same scorn

will be waiting for you: if you leave me, my prayer will be
    paid for,
        nothing you offer will ever atone.
Though you must hurry, this is a slight delay; after three
    handfuls of earth, you may be on your way.

Well, Iccius, do you envy the Arabs
their treasure, are you mapping an all-out war
    on Sabaean kings who have never
        been conquered, are your chains all ready for

the dreadful Mede? And will a foreign virgin,
once you have killed her lover, become your slave?
    Will a boy from the palace, perfume
        on his hair, taught with papa's bow to shoot

oriental arrows, will he be appointed
your cupbearer? Who will say that the rivers
    cannot halt their descent and flow up
        tall mountains, and Tiber run in reverse,

when you persist in trading Panaetius'
treatises, picked up all over the city,
    and the Socratic school for Spanish
        armor? We looked for better things from you.

O Venus, who rule over Cnidos and Paphos,
leave your favorite Cyprus for the charming
shrine where Glycera offers much incense
 and prays for your coming.

May your burning boy come swiftly with you
and the Graces in flowing robes and the Nymphs
and Youth who has no grace without you
 and Mercury too.

What does the poet ask at Apollo's new
temple? What is his prayer, as he pours new wine
    from the bowl? Not for the abounding
        harvests of fertile Sardinia,

not for pleasant herds in sultry Calabria,
not for gold and ivory from India,
    not for fields that the silent Liris
        nibbles with its easy waters.

Let them prune their vines in Cales, those
to whom Fortune grants it, so the wealthy trader
    may drink deep from golden bowls
        wines bought with Syrian goods:

that man the gods must love: each year he returns
three or four times to the Atlantic ocean
    unharmed. As for me, I feast on olives,
        endives, a light diet of mallows.

Apollo, give me joy in what I have,
I pray, and with good health and a steady mind,
    may my old age be spent without
        dishonor, and not be deprived of the lyre.

I · 32

A poem's requested. If ever I dallied in
the shade with you, toying with songs that will live
this year and thereafter, come, play a Roman
    lyric, my lyre,

first strummed by Alcaeus, the man of Lesbos,
a brave soldier in war, but in a battle,
or in a battered ship off a wave-washed coast
    riding at anchor,

he would sing of Bacchus, the Muses, Venus
and the boy who is forever by her side,
and Lycus, beautiful, for his eyes are dark,
    and dark is his hair.

O lyre that graces Apollo, that gladdens
the high feasts of Jove, O gentle medicine
when minds are troubled, hear me whenever I
    fitly invoke you.

Albius, stop upsetting yourself by brooding
over hardhearted Glycera, stop singing these
endless complaints: why does a younger man now catch
    her eye, why did she break her word?

Love has Lycoris, praised for a beautiful brow,
burning up for Cyrus, Cyrus turns her down
for cold-shouldering Pholoe, but sooner shall
    does mate with Apulian wolves

than Pholoe shall sin with so coarse a lover.
That is the way Venus wants it; she likes a joke
that hurts: bodies and souls with nothing in common
    must bear her unbreakable yoke.

It happened to me: once when a more noble Venus
wanted me, I was held by the charming chains
of Myrtale, once a slave, and rougher than waves
    off the Cape of Calabria.

Seldom I paid my cheap respects to the gods
those off-course years when I had my degree in
    fool's philosophy; now I must set
        the sails for my voyage back, and follow

the route I rejected: for God the Father,
whose flashes of lightning often split a sky
    full of clouds, this time down the clear air
        drove his swift wheels and thundering horses;

and the steady ground and the flowing waters,
the Styx and the dreaded hellgate Taenarus,
    the end of the earth where Atlas stands,
        felt it and shook. The god is powerful:

highest for lowest he changes; a great man
goes down as an unknown rises; one man hears
    Fortune whirl her shrill wings and his crown
        is gone; she's pleased to place it on this one.

Fortune, goddess who rules lovely Antium,
who have power to lift our timebound bodies
    from the lowest condition, or turn
        triumphal processions to funerals,

the poor tenant farmer begs you to help him
in troubled prayers, you are petitioned
    as queen of the sea by those who dare
        Aegean waves in Bithynian ships,

the savage Dacian, the Scythian nomad
pray to you, towns and tribes and belligerent
    Latium, and foreign queen mothers
        and purple-robed tyrants plead in terror

that the standing pillar may not be thrust down
by your terrible foot, that the rebel mob
    may not spur the more prudent "to arms,
        to arms," and shatter the ruling power.

Always before you walks harsh Necessity:
she is carrying joining nails and wedges
    in her brazen hand, and she does not
        forget the strict clamp and the molten lead.

You are dear to Hope; and Loyalty, whose hand
is wrapped in white cloth, who is found so seldom,
    does not withdraw her friendship when you
        grow cold and leave a great house in mourning.

But the crowd is not loyal, and a mistress
will leave in spite of her vows, and friends wander
    off, once they have emptied the storeroom,
        liars who bear no part of the burden.

Keep Caesar safe when he marches on Britain
at the end of the earth, and the new conscripts,
    young men who will teach the fear of Rome
        to the Eastern tribes along the Red Sea.

O we bear the disgrace of scars and crimes and
brothers—we are the tough ones: is there anything
    we have turned from doing? an evil
        we have not touched? have our young people once

feared the gods enough to keep hands off? is there
one sanctuary they respect? O hammer
    our blunted swords on a new anvil
        to use against Scythians and Arabs.

With incense and with music and the
    proper offering of a young bull's blood, let us
thank the gods who guard Numida,
    who has now come safe home from the far Western
    lands,

with kisses for many close friends,
    but for none of them more than for his Lamia,
the dearest, when he remembers their
    young days with the same tutor, and the time they both

put on the togas of manhood.
    Mark this up as a red-letter day, no limit
to the wine jars you bring from the
    storeroom, not a pause between Salian dances,

and may strongheaded Damalis
    lose to Bassus their Thracian battle in wine.
Let our banquet have roses and
    long-lasting parsley and lilies that fade so soon.

All eyes will sicken with longing
    as they linger over Damalis, but her new
lover has all her attention,
    and she clings to him closer than wanton ivy.

Now for a drinking spree, now for a loose-footed
light fantastic, now is the time to pay
    our debt to the gods, my friends,
        and spread a spectacular banquet.

Before today, to bring the Caecuban from
family storerooms was wrong, while the crazy
    queen was still scheming with her
        sickly eunuchs, her pack of perverts,

to send the Capitol crashing and bury
the empire: wild were her dreams of doing
    whatever she wished, the best
        luck was her liquor. She sobered up

when her ships caught fire, scarcely one unscathed,
and delusions of mind nursed on Egypt's wine
    were cured by Caesar with the facts
        of fear, his navy close as she fled

from Italy, like a hawk going after
a gentle dove, or a swift hunter tracking
    a hare over snow-covered fields
        in Thessaly: chains awaited this

damnable monster. But a heroine's death
was her goal: she showed no female shivers
    at the sight of a sword, and her
        fast-sailing fleet sought no secret harbors.

Her courage was great: she looked on her fallen
palace, a smile still on her face, and boldly
    played with venomous serpents,
        her flesh drinking their bitter poison,

so highly she dared, her mind set on her death.
Not for her the enemy ship, the crownless
    voyage, her role in the grand
        parade: she was no weak-kneed woman.

I'm bothered, boy, by Persian elegance,
expensive garlands are not to my taste;
stop searching through hidden spots where late
    roses linger.

I want no fuss, nothing added to plain
myrtle garlands: myrtle suits us both,
you as you serve, me as I drink, beneath
    the close-leaved vine.

II · 1

Civic unrest since Metellus was consul,
and causes and crimes and stages of the war,
    and Fortune's toying, and powerful
        coalitions of leaders, and weapons

smeared with blood that is still not expiated,
a field that is filled with the risk of danger,
    this is your topic, and you walk on
        fires that lurk beneath deceptive ashes.

A brief while only may the solemn tragic
Muse be missing from the stage: soon, Pollio,
    your history composed, return to
        the high vocation of Greek tragedy.

You are known for your help to troubled clients
and to the Senate in its council chamber,
    and your victory in Dalmatia
        gave you the laurel's eternal glory.

And now you batter our ears with the horns'
clangor of horror, now the clarions cry,
    now the weapons glitter and fear grows
        in gutless horses and riders' faces;

now I seem to hear the mighty commanders
defiled with the dirt that is no dishonor

and of all the world lying conquered
except the fiery heart of Cato.

Juno and other gods, who were partial to
Africa, and who left the land they could not
avenge, offer the victors' grandsons
as victims at the tomb of Jugurtha.

Is there a field not fertile with Latin blood,
that will not speak with its graves of unholy
battles, and of the crash of the West
in ruins, as the Parthians listened?

Is there a gorge or a river not touched by war
and its sorrows? Is there a sea that has not
been discolored by slaughtered Romans?
Is there a shore that has not seen our blood?

But my Muse, you are reckless, forsaking play,
trying for the part of a writer of dirges:
come with me into Venus' cavern
to look for lighter music for the strings.

Silver that is hidden in the greedy ground
has no shine, Sallustius Crispus, and you
have no liking for metal unless it gleams
    with sensible use.

The name of Proculeius will always live
who acted as a father to his brothers:
the unfaltering wings of long-lasting Fame
    will carry him on.

If your greed is conquered, you have dominions
greater than if you linked distant Cadiz to
Libya, and Carthaginians in both
    served the same ruler.

Dropsy grows worse, the more a person gives in,
and you cannot get rid of thirst till the veins
are free of its curse, and the pallid body
    of water's weakness.

Phraates has returned to the throne of Cyrus:
Virtue never runs with the crowd, and will not
list him as happy, and she teaches people
    not to use the wrong

words: she gives power and a crown that is safe
and long-lasting laurels to that man alone
who can see great mountains of treasure and not
    look back with longing.

Keep this in mind: a steady head on a steep
path; the same holds true when the going is good:
    don't let happiness go to your head,
        friend Dellius, for you must die someday,

whether you spend all your time in sorrowing,
or keep yourself happy on festival days
    stretched out on the grass in seclusion
        with a jar of your best Falernian.

Why do the towering pine and white poplar
love to weave shady welcome by lacing their
    branches? Why do the rushing waters
        hurry on against the winding river?

Tell them to bring the wines and the perfumes and
sweet rose blossoms that live such a little while,
    here, while it still is allowed by luck and
        youth, and the dark threads of the three sisters.

You will leave the pastures you bought and your home
and your country place washed by yellow Tiber,
    you will leave, and into the hands of
        an heir go the riches you piled so high.

Rich, and descended from ancient Inachus,
or poor and from the lowest class, loitering
    out in the open, it is all one:
        an offering to Death, who has no tears.

All of us are being herded there, for all
lots are tossing in an urn: sooner, later,
        out they will come and book our passage
        on the boat for everlasting exile.

No need to blush for your love of a slave girl,
Xanthias of Phocis. In earlier days
Briseis the slave, her skin like snow, aroused
    aloof Achilles;

Ajax, the son of Telamon, was mastered
by the beauty of his captive Tecmessa;
as he conquered, the fire seized Atreus' son
    for a captured girl,

after the armies of Troy had succumbed to
Achilles' triumph, and the loss of Hector
handed Ilium, now an easy victim,
    to the weary Greeks.

For all that you know, your golden-haired Phyllis
has wealthy parents, credits to their new son;
her blood must be royal, and she laments for
    her gods' unkindness.

Believe me, this girl you adore does not come
from nasty commoners: no, such loyalty,
such disdain for money, could not be born of
    a shameful mother.

Her arms and her face and her smooth slender legs
win my cool approval. Have no fear of me,
whose life has already gone hurrying past
    its fortieth year.

No, she is not yet able to stand the yoke
on her yielding neck, not able to do her
  share of the job, or to take the shock
    of the bull's rush in the act of coupling.

The thoughts of your little heifer are all on
green meadows: at times she finds in the water
  relief from the heat, at times she longs
    to frolic with other heifers among

the moist willows. Get rid of your craving for
grapes out of season: only a little while,
  and, just for you, pied autumn will dye
    the darkening clusters a deep purple.

A little while, and she follows you, for time
races on unchecked, adding to her the years
  taken from you, a little while, and
    Lalage boldly comes for her husband:

you will love her far more than shy Pholoe,
more than Chloris, her white shoulders as glowing
  as clear moonlight shining from the sea
    at midnight, more than Gyges from Cnidos,

who could mingle with a group of young girls and amaze
the shrewdest strangers when they failed to choose him,
  concealed by his hair that flows freely
    and his face that might be a boy's or girl's.

Septimius, who would travel with me to
Cadiz and unsubjected Cantabria
and uncivilized Syrtes, where Moorish waves
    surge incessantly:

Tibur, founded by pioneers from Argos,
there is the place I would be in my old age,
there is my rest when weary of sea and roads
    and a soldier's life.

If the unkind Fates say I cannot stay there,
I will go to the river Galaesus, dear
to the sheep who wear skins, and fields once ruled by
    Spartan Phalanthus.

That part of the world has a welcome for me
beyond all others, where the honey equals
that of Hymettus, and olives rival the
    green of Venafrum,

where the spring is long and the winters are mild
thanks to Jupiter, and Aulon, favored by
Bacchus' fertility, does not envy the
    grapes of Falernum.

That is the place whose blessed hills are calling
for you as for me; there you will shed the tears
proper to grief, above the warm ashes of
    your friend, the poet.

O many the rough spots with you beside me,
led there by Brutus when he led the army:
    who has restored you to civil rights,
        your country's gods and Italian skies,

Pompeius? You were the first of my close friends;
many a dragging day I broke up with you
    and with wine, garlands upon my hair
        that glistened with ointment from Syria.

I went through Philippi and panic with you,
behaving badly, leaving my shield behind,
    when Valor was smashed and threatening
        troops ended up with foul dirt in their mouths.

But I, scared stiff, was carried by Mercury
in a thick cloud quickly through enemy lines;
    you were.carried back by the wave to
        war, and off upon its troubled waters.

Then offer to Jove the feast that you vowed him,
and deposit your legs, that are sick of long
    service, under my laurel, and don't
        go slow on the wine I've reserved for you.

Fill up the gleaming leafy cups with Massic,
wine that helps us forget, pour out the ointments
    from the deep jars. Which of you boys will
        hurry to weave us garlands of pliant

parsley or myrtle? What do the dice say, who
is master of the revels? I will riot less
      sanely than Thracians: a friend is back
          with me, and it's good to go on a spree.

If just once in return for your perjured vows
something hurt you, Barine, as you deserve,
if a single tooth or fingernail blackened
    to spoil your beauty,

I would trust you. But soon as your faithless head
is jeopardized with oaths, you glow more brightly,
lovelier than ever: you come in as the boys'
    feature attraction.

It does you a world of good to swear falsehoods
by your mother's buried ashes, night's silent
stars, heaven itself, and the gods who never
    know death and its cold.

Really, Venus herself is laughing; the simple
Nymphs are laughing, and uncivilized Cupid,
who is always sharpening burning arrows
    on a bloodstained stone.

What's more, the boys are all growing up for you,
a new band of slaves is growing, but the old
do not leave the home of their fickle mistress,
    despite frequent threats.

You are feared by mothers of adolescents,
by stingy fathers, by worried brides, virgins
only a while ago, whose husbands may be
    held in your aura.

Showers do not fall from clouds to soggy fields
forever, and the Caspian Sea is not
    always tossing and roughed up with storms,
        and on the frontiers of Armenia,

friend Valgius, the ice does not stand fixed fast
every month, and Mount Garganus' oak forests
    are not always thrashed by northern winds
        and its ash trees forever stripped of leaves:

you go on forever in mournful meters
of your loss of Mystes, and the evening star
    does not silence your lovesongs by rising
        or running away from the racing sun.

But Nestor, who lasted three generations,
did not weep for his dear Antilochus all
    the rest of his years, and the Trojan
        parents and sisters of boyish Troilus

did not cry forever. Turn at last from these
soft lamentations, and let us have stronger
    music for Augustus Caesar's new
        victories, for icebound Mount Niphates

and the Euphrates, running a little less
rapidly, with the Medes listed as conquered,
    and the Geloni, kept in limits,
        galloping across their restricted plains.

Better to live, Licinius, not always
rushing into deep water, and not, when fear
of storms makes you shiver, pushing too close to
     the dangerous coast.

A man who prizes golden moderation
stays safely clear of the filth of a run-down
building, stays prudently out of a palace
     others will envy.

The giant pine is more often troubled by the
wind, and the tallest towers collapse with a
heavier fall, and bolts of lightning strike the
     tops of the mountains.

Hopeful in the bad times, fearful in the good times,
that is the man who has readied his heart for
the turn of the dice. Jupiter brings back foul
     winters; he also

takes them away. No, if things are bad now, they
will not remain that way: sometimes Apollo
wakes the silent Muse with his lyre and is not
     always an archer.

When troubles come, show that you have a stout heart
and a stern face: but see that you have the good sense
to take in sail when it swells in a wind that's
    a little too kind.

Stop brooding, Quinctius, over foreign affairs,
what warmongers overseas are scheming
    East and West. Don't fret about
        the cost of living: it's small really.

Behind us youth, its glow and grace, runs out;
age and its wrinkles will put to rout
    love's fun and games and easy sleep.
        Spring blossoms do not hold their pride

forever, nor has the moon that is glowing now
a single face. Why exhaust yourself, Quinctius?
    You're not up to perpetual planning.
        Why not relax beneath this tall

plane tree or pine, grey hair crowned with
sweet roses, sprinkled with Syrian balsam,
    and drink while we can? The winegod
        drives worry away. Which slave will mix

spring water and strong wine? Who will coax
that shy lay, Lyde, from home? Tell her to
    hurry, and bring her ivory lyre:
        her hair is done in the latest style.

You would not enjoy it if the lengthy warfare
with fierce Numantia, or stubborn Hannibal,
or the sea of Sicily red with Punic blood
    were set to the lyre's soft music,

or the wild Lapithae and Hylaeus gone mad
with wine, or the taming of giant sons of Earth
at the hands of Hercules, when their threats shook the
    shining house of ancient Saturn

with fear: you are the man and prose the medium
for a history telling of Caesar's battles,
Maecenas, and of the once belligerent kings
    led by their necks through the city.

But I, under Muse's orders, must celebrate
the lovely singing of Lady Licymnia,
her clear, sparkling eyes, and her heart that keeps so well
    its promise of love in return,

who played a graceful part in the choral dancing
and the dialogue and offered her arms to
the maidens adorned for the celebration on
    Diana's crowded holy day.

Would you trade for all of Achaemenes' riches
or the wealth of Midas in fertile Phrygia
or the fully packed houses in Arabia
    a curl of Licymnia's hair,

when she bends her head for your passionate kisses
or teases you cruelly and will not have them?
She likes, even more than you, to have them stolen;
    sometimes she steals them first herself.

He planted you a day the omens were dark,
whoever he was, and his defiling hands
    raised you as a tree to destroy his
        descendants and disgrace the neighborhood.

He was, I should think, a man who would crush
his own father's throat and at midnight spatter
    the sanctuary of home with the
        blood of a guest; and he had dealings in

Colchic poisons and every conceivable
kind of vice, that man who stood you on my farm,
    sad excuse for a tree, to fall on
        the head of your undeserving owner.

Men are never careful enough, day to day,
of what to avoid: the Punic sailor is
    afraid of the Bosphorus, but has
        no fear of what may be hiding beyond;

the soldier is scared of Parthian tactics
of shoot and run, Parthians of Italy's
    chains and toughness; but unforeseen the
        force of death has gripped and will grip all men.

How close I came to seeing the kingdom of
dark Proserpina, and Aeacus' courtroom,
    the places set apart for the just,
        and Sappho singing to Aeolian

lyre of the coldhearted girls of her country,
and you, Alcaeus, making stronger music
  and chanting of your hard life at sea,
    bitter hard times in exile, hard fighting.

And the shades wonder at the poems of each
that earn an awed silence; but to slake their ears
  with battles and tyrants driven out
    they crowd more thickly, shoulder to shoulder.

Is it any wonder, when their songs can lull
the many-headed beast until his black ears
  droop, and the snakes have time for a rest
    from writhing in the hair of the Furies?

And even Prometheus and Tantalus
find the pleasing sound a distraction from pain,
  and Orion does not keep his mind
    on hunting lions and cautious lynxes.

Ah god how they race, Postumus, Postumus,
how the years run out, and doing what is right
    will not delay wrinkles and age's
        onslaught and death who cannot be beaten;

no, dear friend, not even if every day
you tried with three hundred bulls to please Pluto,
    who has no tears, who holds in prison
        three-bodied Geryon and Tityos

by the sorrowful river whose crossing is
certain for those who live by the gifts of the earth,
    a must for all, the high and mighty
        and the poverty-stricken small farmers.

It will do no good to escape bloody Mars
and breaking waves on the rough Adriatic,
    it will do no good to spend autumn
        in terror of sirocco and sickness:

we must see the dark waters of Cocytos
winding slowly, and the infamous daughters
    of Danaus, and Sisyphus, son of
        Aeolus, condemned to endless labor.

We must leave behind us earth and home and dear
wife, and of all the trees that you care for now,
    not one will follow you, so briefly
        its master, only the loathsome cypress.

An heir who deserves it will drink Caecuban
you kept safe with a hundred keys, and he will
    soak the floor with magnificent wine,
        finer than the priests drink at their festivals.

There will soon be few acres left for a plow
by these splendid heaps; all around you will see
    ponds for fish stretching wider than Lake
        Lucrine, and the solitary plane tree

will oust the ivied elms: then violet-beds
and myrtles and all that enriches the nose
    will spread their perfumes where olive groves
        grew richly once for the former owner.

Then the dense branches of laurel will cut off
the sun's hot rays. When Romulus and long-haired
    Cato and ancestral tradition
        ruled over us, things like this were not done.

In their days the private holdings were little,
the public large: no portico with northern
    exposure, measured in ten-foot lengths,
        was possessed by a private citizen;

their way of life did not let them disdain the
sod when it came in handy, but it made them
    beautify at public cost their towns
        and temples to the gods with rare marble.

Peace, he begs of the gods, caught on the open
Aegean, with black clouds holding the moon in
hiding, and the stars no longer steadily
    shining for sailors;

peace is the prayer of battle-maddened Thrace;
peace, beg Parthians with their painted quivers:
it is not bought, Grosphus, with purple cloths, with
    jewels or with gold.

No, neither royal treasures nor a consul's
lictor can clear the crowd of worries away
from the mind, and the troubles that flutter near
    the paneled ceilings.

He lives well with little, the man whose fathers'
salt dish shines on his impoverished table,
and whose easy sleep is not stolen by fear
    or by filthy greed.

Why do we try for so much so hard with such
little time? Why do we turn to countries warmed
by a different sun? What exile from home
    escapes himself too?

The disease of worry boards the bronze-prowed ship,
and troops of horsemen cannot leave it behind,
swifter than stags and swifter than the Eastwind
    driving the stormclouds.

Joyful here and now, may the spirit despise
concern for what lies beyond and dilute the
bitter with a calm smile. Nothing is wholly
    filled with happiness.

Sudden death took Achilles in his glory,
his long old age wasted Tithonus away,
and to me perhaps this hour will offer
    what you are denied.

You are surrounded by a hundred mooing
herds of Sicilian cattle, you can hear
your racehorse whinny, you are dressed in wool
    double-dyed with Af-

rican purple; I was not cheated by Fate,
who gave me a little farm and a spirit
sensitive to Grecian poetry, above
    the crowd and its spite.

Why must you kill me with all your complaining?
Neither the gods nor I would be pleased if you
    passed away before me, Maecenas,
        the great honor and pillar of my life.

Ah, if too soon an attack should steal your part
of my soul, why would I stay with what is left,
    not worth as much and no longer a
        whole man? One day will bring destruction for

both of us. I have not taken a faithless
oath of allegiance: we will go, we will go,
    whenever you lead the way, ready
        to enjoy as friends the final journey.

I will never be torn from your side, not by
fire-breathing Chimaera nor resurrected
    hundred-handed Gyas: this is the
        will of the Fates and of mighty Justice.

Whether Libra or terrible Scorpio
or Capricorn, ruler of the Western seas,
    was the strongest sign in the hour of
        my birth and casts its influence on me,

in the strangest fashion the stars for us two
have conspired. For you the protection of Jove
    blazing out against Saturn's evil
        was salvation, and held back the beating

wings of Fate, that time the crowded audience
shook the theater three times with joyful applause;
    I, with a tree trunk collapsing to
        brain me, was almost under when Faunus

deflected the blow with his hand: he protects
Mercury's poets. Remember to offer
    sacrifices and a votive shrine;
        I shall spill the blood of a simple lamb.

Not a gold and ivory
        ceiling can cast a reflection in my home;
not a marble beam from Mount
        Hymettus weighs down pillars dug far

off in Africa; I'm no
        surprise heir who camps in Attalus' palace,
and no well-bred ladies, robed
        in Laconian purple, attend on me.

But for me, trust, and a full
        vein of talent, and poor as I am the rich
come to find me: I demand
        nothing more from the gods, and exact no greater

favors from a friend in power,
        blissful enough with my one and only farm.
Day is crowding after day,
        and the new moons are hurrying on to wane:

you contract for marble slabs
        at the brink of burial, and heap up a
mansion, not a thought of tombs,
        and push on the work of extending the shore

into Baiae's roaring sea,
        not owning enough while the coast confines you.
Then the posts that mark the bounds
        of your holdings are rooted up: lusting for

more, you jump the claims of your
    tenant farmers. They are driven off, wife and
husband, and they carry their
    household gods and scrawny children in their arms.

Yet there is no hall that waits
    more surely for a master of property
than the predetermined bounds
    of greedy Death. Why strain for more? Impartial

earth is open to the poor
    and to prince's sons, and the servant of Death
took no gold to ferry back
    clever Prometheus. He holds confined proud

Tantalus and Tantalus'
    descendants, he brings release to the poor man
when he finishes the job,
    and he hears him, whether he is called or not.

Bacchus on the far-off rocky hills, teaching
his chants—you who are still to come, believe me—
    I saw him and his student Nymphs and
        goat-footed Satyrs and their pointed ears.

Euhoe, my soul trembles with that moment's fear,
Bacchus possesses my breast and I madly
    rejoice. Euhoe, save, god of freedom,
        save me, god of the fearful rod of power.

I must celebrate your inexhaustible
revelers, and the fountains of wine and full
    rivers of milk, and mirror in song
        honey dripping from the hollows of trees;

I must celebrate your blessed bride and her
constellated crown, and Pentheus' palace
    shaken to bits in no small downfall,
        and the finish of Lycurgus of Thrace.

You control the streams, the uncivilized sea,
you are hot with wine as on distant hilltops
    you bind Bistonian women's hair
        with a knot of vipers that does no harm.

And when the rebellious army of giants
tried to climb the heights to the Father's kingdom,
    you were the one who threw back Rhoetus
        and his terrible lion's claws and teeth;

although you were said to be more suitable
for dances and fun and games and were labeled
    unfit for a battle, yet you took
        your part in war as well as in peacetime.

You were graced with golden horn when Cerberus
saw you: he was harmless, and softly wagged his
    tail, and as you were leaving, he licked
        your legs and feet with all three of his tongues.

No paltry or commonplace wings will loft me
through the fluent air in my doubled form as
    a poet, and I will not linger
        longer on earth: high above envy I

will leave the cities. Not for me, the child of
impoverished parents, not for me, your guest,
    my dearest Maecenas, the dying
        and the confinement by the river Styx.

Now, now, the skin on my legs is becoming
wrinkled, and above I am metamorphosed
    to a white bird, and soft feathers are
        forming upon my fingers and shoulders.

Now more famous than Daedalus' Icarus
as a singing bird I will see the shores of
    the roaring Bosphorus, the gulfs of
        Syrtes, and the Hyperborean fields.

I will be known by Colchians and Dacians
(who hide their fear of Marsian troops) and far-off
    Geloni, I will be studied by
        Spanish scholars and the tribes on the Rhone.

Please omit dirges and lamentations and
disgusting grief at my foolish funeral;
    keep down the clamor and never mind
        the superfluous tribute of a tomb.

III · 1

I scorn the secular crowd and keep them out.
Be silent. I am a priest of the Muses
   and I chant for young men and maidens
      poems that have never been heard before.

Terrible kings have power over their herds,
over kings themselves is the power of Jove,
   glorious conqueror of Titans,
      shaking all things by raising his eyebrow.

This is so: one man sets out vineyards larger
than another's; one of higher birth comes down
   to the field of Mars, a candidate,
      another contests with better record

and reputation, a third has a bigger
mob of supporters; Necessity's just law
   casts the lots of highest and lowest:
      the urn is large, tossing every name.

The men above whose evil necks a naked
sword is hanging, for them Sicilian banquets
   will not keep their delicious flavor,
      and the music of birds and lyres will not

bring back their sleep. Easy sleep does not despise
the simple homes of the country laborers
    and the shady bank of a river,
        nor any Tempe stirring in the breeze.

The man who longs for just enough is never
disturbed by the turbulent ocean, nor by
    the storm's wild attack when Arcturus
        is setting, or when Haedus is rising,

not by hail that savagely flogs his vineyards,
and his farm's deception, the trees blaming now
    the rains, now the Dog Star that burns up
        the fields, now the unkindness of winters.

The fish feel the waters shrink as the pilings
of stone are laid in the depths; the contractor
    and his crew of slaves toss rubble in,
        under the eyes of the master who loathes

the land. But Anxiety and Dangers climb
to the very same place as the master, and
    black Worry does not leave the bronze-prowed
        trireme, and she clings to the rider's back.

If, then, a troubled man is not consoled by
Phrygian marble, nor living in purple
    more splendid than the stars, nor by wine
        from Falernum and nard from Persia,

why should I erect a palace, with columns
that others would envy, in the latest style?
    Why should I trade my Sabine valley
        for the heavier burden of riches?

Let him learn to suffer poverty's strictness
gladly, a young man toughened by hard army
　　　training, and be a horseman whose spear
　　　　　is feared, a plague to savage Parthians,

and spend his life under the sky in danger
and action. Watching from the enemy walls,
　　　may the wife of the warring ruler
　　　　　and the virgin who is ripe for marriage

sigh: "Ah god, our royal lover knows little
of battles, may he not arouse the lion
　　　who is wild when touched, whose thirst for blood
　　　　　drives him on through the heart of the slaughter."

Precious and proper is death for one's country.
And death comes swiftly after the runaway
　　　and shows no mercy to the hamstrings
　　　　　and the boneless backs of peace-loving boys.

Manhood, that has known no disgrace in defeat,
retains its brightness, its honors untarnished,
　　　and does not take or leave the axes
　　　　　at the whim of the wavering public.

Manhood, that to those who do not deserve death
opens heaven, takes a path barred to others
　　　and turns away on its beating wings
　　　　　from the mere masses and the muddy earth.

And there is certain reward for the silence
that keeps faith: I will forbid one who broadcasts
 the secret rites of Ceres to stay
  beneath the same roof, or cast off with me

in a thin ship; God the Father, disobeyed,
has often put innocent in with guilty:
 seldom, with the sinner in the lead,
  does Punishment fail though its feet are lame.

When a man is just and firm in his purpose,
the citizens burning to approve a wrong
    or the frowning looks of a tyrant
        do not shake his fixed mind, nor the Southwind,

wild lord of the uneasy Adriatic,
nor the thunder in the mighty hand of Jove:
    should the heavens crack and tumble down,
        as the ruins crushed him he would not fear.

This was why Pollux and roaming Hercules,
climbing hard, came at last to the blazing heights,
    with whom Augustus will take his ease,
        sipping the nectar with his crimson lips.

This, Father Bacchus, was why you merited
a team of tigers, their untrained necks pulling
    in harness; this was why Romulus
        fled from Acheron behind Mars' horses

when the gods were in council and Juno spoke
words that were welcome: "Ilium, Ilium,
    a corrupted and death-bringing judge
        and an alien woman have turned you

to dust: once Laomedon cheated the gods
of the gifts he had promised, you were surrendered
    to me and to virgin Minerva,
        with your people and their deceitful king.

Now the notorious guest does not preen for
his Spartan adultress, and the oath-breaking
house of Priam, strengthened by Hector,
does not break the line of Greek soldiers,

and the war that our quarrels drew out so long
has subsided. From now on, I will give up
my great wrath and my hated grandson,
who was born to the high priestess of Troy,

back to Mars; I will permit him to enter
the regions of light, to discover the taste
of nectar, and to be enrolled as
one of the peaceful company of gods.

Just as long as between Rome and Ilium
a broad sea rages, may the refugees be
happy, ruling wherever they please;
as long as the cattle trample upon

the grave of Priam and Paris, and wild beasts
hide the young there unharmed, may the Capitol
stand and shine, and may warfaring Rome
lay down the law to conquered Parthians.

May her name, striking widespread terror, expand
to the farthest shores, where a stretch of water
separates Europe from Africa,
where the swelling Nile nourishes the fields:

she will have more power in turning away from
unmined gold, better off when earth still holds it,
than in gathering it for men's use
with a hand that defiles all that's holy.

Whatever the limit that confines the world,
this may her soldiers touch, yearning to look on
    places that are gripped by burning heat
        or by low-hanging clouds and ceaseless rain.

But I prophesy for warrior Romans
on one condition: never must excessive
    devotion or overconfidence
        make them wish to rebuild ancestral Troy.

The fortune of Troy, born again with evil
omens, would come once more to sorry ruin,
    with myself, wife and sister to Jove,
        commanding the conquering regiments.

If three times the city's brazen wall should rise,
built by Phoebus, three times it shall fall, destroyed
    by my Greeks, three times the captured wife
        shall lament for her man and her children."

But this is not suited to a playful lyre:
Muse, what are you up to? Put an end to this
    foolish attempt at the words of gods,
        shrinking major themes to minor meters.

Come down from the sky, Calliope, goddess,
sing to the flute a long-lasting melody,
    or with clear voice alone, if you wish,
        or to the strings of the lyre of Phoebus.

Do you hear her too, or does a delightful
madness trick me? I seem to hear her, and to
    wander through sacred groves, under whose
        branches flow pleasant breezes and waters.

When I was a boy, on pathless Mount Vultur,
off limits laid down by Pullia, my nurse,
    and worn out with playing and sleepy,
        the doves of legend wove me a blanket

of fresh-fallen leaves, a wonder to all who
live in the nest of high Acherontia,
    and the forest of Bantia, and the
        fertile fields of lowlying Forentum,

how I slept, my body safe from the deadly
vipers and the bears, how I was covered with
    heaps of myrtle and sacred laurel,
        a child unafraid, favored by the gods.

Yours, O Muses, yours as I climb the steep
Sabine hills, or find it pleasant to visit
    the chill of Praeneste, or the slopes
        of Tibur, or the clear air of Baiae.

Lover of your springs and your choral dances,
I was not killed when the ranks at Philippi
    broke and ran, nor by that hellbent tree,
        nor by the waves off Point Palinurus.

As long as you are with me, I shall gladly
be a mariner daring the Bosphorus'
    rages, or a traveler over
        the scorching sands of the Syrian coast;

I shall see the British, so fierce to strangers,
and the Concani who like to drink horseblood,
    I shall see Gelonian quivers
        and Scythia's river, and stay unharmed.

Noble Caesar, after he settles in towns
the soldiers who are tired out from campaigning,
    longing to finish his own labors,
        finds your Pierian cave refreshing.

You give gentle wisdom, and rejoice in the
giving, benevolent sisters. We know that
    evil Titans and their monstrous mob
        were struck by a bolt of lightning falling

from him who controls motionless earth, wind-tossed
ocean, and the cities and sorrow's kingdom,
    the one who rules in just supremacy
        over the gods and the nations of men.

A mighty terror was inflicted on Jove
by those bold upstarts and their horrible hands,
    and the brothers straining to impose
        Mount Pelion upon dark Olympus.

But what could Typhoeus and forceful Minos,
or what Porphyrion's threatening stance,
        what could Rhoetus, and Enceladus
            who dared to root up the trees and hurl them,

achieve by their assault on the clangorous
shield of Pallas? There stood Vulcan, hungry for
        the battle, here was Juno the wife,
            and he whose bow never leaves his shoulder,

who bathes his unbound hair with Castalia's
pure springwater, who rules the Lycian woods
        and the groves of his island birthplace,
            Delos' and Patara's god, Apollo.

Without wisdom, power falls of its own weight:
under control, power is increased to more
        by the gods themselves; but they despise
            power wholeheartedly used for evil.

As proof of my pronouncement, hundred-handed
Gyas, and the notorious Orion
        who assaulted maiden Diana
            and was mastered by her virgin arrows.

Earth, heaped over her monstrous offspring, laments,
and weeps for children flung by the thunderbolt
        to the dim world of Death; the swift flames
            have not consumed the burden of Etna,

and the vulture, appointed to guard his lust,
has not abandoned the liver of unchaste
        Tityos; love-possessed Pirithous
            is held in restraint by three hundred chains.

Thunder from heaven and faith is confirmed in
Jove's dominion; a god on earth we shall call
　　　Augustus, who joins to the empire
　　　　　　the British and troublesome Parthians.

And did Crassus' soldiers live as the shameful
husbands of barbarian wives, and grow old
　　　—O perversion of the Roman way—
　　　　　　in arms for enemy in-laws, under

Parthian rule, Apulian and Marsian
blotting out the sacred shields and the name and
　　　the toga, and eternal Vesta,
　　　　　　while Jove's temple stood, and Rome, the City?

Farsighted Regulus guarded against this,
refusing to accept the disgraceful terms
　　　of peace, and to set an example
　　　　　　that would spread ruin through the years to come,

if young men taken captive did not perish
unpitied. "Our banners hanging in Punic
　　　sanctuaries, weapons torn without
　　　　　　bloodshed from soldiers: I myself," he said,

"have seen these things, I have seen myself the arms
of citizens bound behind their freeborn backs,
　　　and the gates no longer barred, and fields
　　　　　　our battles ruined being plowed once more.

If gold buys them back, why surely the soldiers
return all the braver to action. You add
    damage to shame: wool dyed in purple
        never recovers the color it lost,

nor does true manhood, when it once disappears,
wish to be restored to those who are weaklings.
    When a doe freed from close-woven nets
        puts up a fight, then he will be brave who

trusted himself to treacherous enemies;
in new wars he will crush Carthaginians
    who did not move when he felt the ropes
        binding back his arms, and who dreaded death.

Ignorant of the way to make life secure,
he diluted war with peace. O the disgrace!
    O mighty Carthage, the shameful
        decline of Italy lifts you higher!"

They say he drew himself back from the kisses
of his virtuous wife and little children
    as if civil rights were gone, and turned
        his stern and manly face towards the ground

until he had toughened the shaky senate
with advice no speaker ever gave before,
    and through the lamentations of friends
        could hurry out, a glorious exile.

And though he knew what the foreign torturer
was preparing for him, yet he pushed aside
    relatives who were blocking his way
        and those who tried to delay his return,

just as if, with a lengthy lawsuit settled,
he were leaving his clients' cases behind,
   taking a trip to Venafrum's fields
      or Tarentum, once settled by Spartans.

III · 6

You, the guiltless, will pay for your fathers' sins,
Roman, until you repair the decaying
    temples and shrines of the gods, and their
        images, filthy with blackening smoke.

When you act as servant of the gods, you rule:
from them all beginning, leave them the ending;
    neglected, the gods have brought many
        sorrows to suffering Italy.

Twice now Monaeses and Pacorus' army,
when omens were evil, have smashed our attack
    to bits, and they grin as they fasten
        our trophies to their skimpy necklaces.

In the grip of civil conflicts the city
was nearly wiped out by Egypt and Dacia,
    the one with a frightening fleet, and
        the other with superior archers.

Breeder of vices, our age has polluted
first marriage vows and the children and the home;
    from this spring, a river of ruin
        has flooded our country and our people.

The blossoming virgin enjoys her course in
Ionic dancing, and even now practices
    all the tricks, and thoughts of sinful loves
        fill her to the tender tips of her toes.

Soon she is after, at her husband's parties,
younger lovers, and is not particular
    about the one she hastily gives
        the forbidden thrills when the lights go out;

then called for, her husband there and knowing it,
she responds, whether a salesman summons her
    or the master of a Spanish ship,
        a wealthy trader in adulteries.

Not from parents like these were the young men born
who stained the sea with Carthaginian blood
    and struck down Pyrrhus and the mighty
        Antiochus and dreadful Hannibal;

no, they were men, the descendants of farm-bred
soldiers, who were raised to turn over the clods
    with their Sabine hoes, and to chop wood
        and carry it in at their stern mother's

orders, as the Sungod shifted the shadows
    the mountains, and gave the weary oxen
      relief from the yoke, bringing an hour
        of rest as his chariot departed.

What does time's decaying leave undiminished?
Our parent's age, worse than their parents', brought forth
    us, who are still worse, who soon will breed
        descendants even more degenerate.

Why these tears, Asterie, for the man whom clear
winds from the West will bring back early in spring
    rich with Bithynian goods,
        the young lover true to his vows,

Gyges? Forced by the Southwind into Oricus
at the time of the mad Star, the Goat, he passes
    the cold nights without sleeping,
        not without a good many tears.

Yet a servant from his solicitous hostess,
reporting that pitiful Chloe sighs and grows
    feverish over your flame,
        tempts him with a thousand sly tricks.

She alludes to the treacherous woman whose false
accusations incited credulous Proetus
    to plan a sudden death for
        Bellerophon, who was too chaste;

she speaks of Peleus, almost in Tartarus
for staying chastely away from Hippolyte,
    and telling him these stories,
        subtly advises him to sin.

No use: for deafer than the cliffs of Icaros
he hears her words and his heart is still whole. But you,
    make sure you are not too pleased
        with your neighbor Enipeus,

even though no one is seen to equal his skill
as he jockeys a mount upon the Field of Mars,
  and no one equals his speed
    swimming downstream in the Tiber.

Lock up the house as night is falling, do not peek
into the street at the tune of his wailing flute,
  and though he often calls you
    hardhearted, just stay hard to get.

III · 8

March the First: I'm single: what am I up to?
What is the meaning of flowers, and censer
filled with incense, and live coals laid on fresh turf?
    Wondering, are you,

you master of learning in either language?
I vowed a white goat and a delicious feast
to Bacchus, that day the tree fell and I was
    nearly put under.

Every year, when this holy day comes around,
it will draw the pitch-sealed cork from a wine jar
put up to absorb the smoke in the year that
    Tullus was consul.

Drink up, Maecenas, a hundred cups to your
friend and his safety, and keep the lights awake
until daylight: let us stay far away from all
    racket and brawling.

Put aside your official civic concerns:
Dacian Cotiso is dead with his army;
the dangerous Medes bring themselves to grief by
    war with each other;

the ancient enemy on the Spanish Coast,
Cantabria, bows, subdued to our fetters;
now the Scythians, bows unstrung, are planning
    to give up their plains.

Take it easy: stop troubling too much over
public welfare: be a private citizen,
joyfully take the gifts of this hour, letting
    the grave matters go.

"As long as I was dear to you,
    and there was no other, a sweeter boy, to put
his arms about your glowing neck,
    I lived more blissful than the king of Persia."

"As long as you burned for no one
    else, and Lydia was not second to Chloe,
Lydia was a noted name
    and I lived more famous than Rome's own Ilia."

"I'm now ruled by Thracian Chloe,
    who knows pretty songs and is clever with a lute,
for whom I would not fear to die
    if the Fates spared my soul and allowed her to live."

"I'm now on fire, and he burns too,
    for Calais, son of Ornytus of Thurii,
for whom I would gladly die twice
    if the Fates spared my boy and allowed him to live."

"What if the early love returned
    and joined those now apart with unbreakable yoke,
if blonde Chloe were brushed aside,
    and the door opened wide for cast-off Lydia?"

"Though he is far more lovely than
    the stars, and you lighter than cork and angrier
than the stormy Adriatic,
    with you I'd love to live, with you I'd gladly die."

Even if you drank from far Tanais, Lyce,
and had married a barbarian, still you would
pity me, dying stretched out before your hard floor
    in the Northwind of your country.

Do you hear how the door is shaking, how the winds
make the trees within the court of your lovely home
moan, and how the fallen snow is freezing over
    as Jupiter rules a clear sky?

Put away your pride, so unpleasing to Venus,
or the rope may run back as the wheel is turning:
your Etrurian parents did not beget a
    Penelope, cold to suitors.

O even if neither presents nor prayers nor
the faces of your lovers, pale and yellowish,
nor your husband's pangs for a whore from Thessaly
    make you yield, spare those who humbly

implore you: you are no softer than rigid oak
and no sweeter at heart than Moroccan vipers.
This body will not put up with your doorstep and
    the rain from the skies forever.

Mercury—for you were the master who taught
Amphion to move the stones with his singing—
and you, the tortoise shell whose seven strings were
    trained to make music,

who once had neither a voice nor grace, but now
please at the rich men's tables and the temples,
play such a song that stubborn Lyde will be
    turning to listen,

for now she leaps like a three-year-old filly
playing in wide meadows, afraid to be touched,
untrained for marriage and not yet ripe for the
    weight of a husband.

You have power to make the tigers and trees
follow you, to call a halt to swift rivers;
the dreadful guardian of the gates of hell,
    Cerberus, yielded

to your charming, although a hundred serpents
stand guard on his terrible head, and a foul
breath and a poisonous spittle flow from his
    mouth and its three tongues.

And even Ixion and Tityos smiled
with painful faces; for a short time the urn
stayed dry, as your welcome music delighted
    Danaus' daughters.

Listen well, Lyde, to the virgins' story
of crime and punishment, of the jar that stays
empty as water runs out through the bottom,
    guilt and the payment,

long delayed, that waited where Death is ruler.
They were evil—what more could they have done—
they were evil, could use the pitiless steel,
    killing their husbands.

Only one, out of so many, was worthy
of her marriage flame, to her faithless father
a glorious traitor: all the ages will
    honor this virgin:

"Arise"—these were her words to her young husband—
"arise, or the long sleep comes on you, from those
you do not fear; escape from my father and
    sin-ridden sisters

who like female lions that have captured calves
tear, ah, their separate prey: I am softer
than they, and I will not strike you, nor lock the
    doors and entrap you.

Let my father heap cruel chains upon me
because I had pity and saved a poor man,
or send me in ships to distant lands, into
    African exile.

Go where your feet and the winds can carry you
while night and Venus are kind; go with heaven's
blessing, and to my memory, on my tomb,
    carve an elegy."

They are in a bad way who cannot let love have its fun, or
   wash
their troubles away with sweet wine, or else must be
   frightened to death
      by a tongue-lashing from uncle.

From you the flying son of Venus takes the woolbasket, from
   you,
Neobule, the weaving and worship of busy Minerva,
      the minute glistening Hebrus

from Lipara has dipped his oiled shoulders in the waves of
   Tiber,
a horseman even better than Bellerophon, never beaten
      for lacking speed of fist or foot,

clever, too, at spearing the deer as they run away in
   frightened
herds across the open plain, and quick to encounter the boar
   who
      hides in the close-woven thickets.

O Bandusia, spring more glittering than glass,
worthy of our gifts of sweet wine and flowers,
    tomorrow a kid will be yours,
        first horns swelling his forehead,

foretelling a life filled with lusting and fighting.
Wasted: for tomorrow this capering kid
    will dye your icy waters
        crimson with his young blood.

In the harsh days when the Dogstar rages
you remain inviolate; to bulls wearied
    with plowing, to roaming
        flocks, a gift of cool pleasure.

You will take your place among the famous springs:
I celebrate the oak that stands above
    your rocks, from your source
        the fall of your clear-voiced waters.

III · 14

Like Hercules, citizens, they said just now
he had sought the laurel at the cost of death:
returning from Spain, seeking his household gods,
    Caesar has conquered.

After sacrifice to the just gods, let his
wife come forth, happy for her matchless husband,
and the sister of our famous leader, and,
    wearing the bands of

suppliants, mothers of young men and maidens
who now are safe. You boys and girls who are still
inexperienced, be sparing with your words,
    speak nothing evil.

For me this day is truly a festival,   ·
driving dark worry away: I fear neither
civil war nor violent death while earth is
    governed by Caesar.

Go, my boy, look for the perfume and garlands
and a jar that recalls the Marsian War,
if a single wine pot was overlooked by
    Spartacus' raiders.

And ask witty Neaera to come quickly,
tying her brown hair back in a simple knot;
if her doorman stays out of sight and creates
    delays, come away.

My hair turns gray, and it softens a spirit
fond of argument and bitter quarreling;
I would not have stood this, when youth was hot and
    Plancus was consul.

III · 15

Wife of that poor man Ibycus,
    put an end for good to your promiscuity
and your scandalous busyness.
    You are close to the right age for burial:

stop playing among the young girls
    and spreading a cloud upon the gleaming white stars.
No, what suits Pholoe is not
    nearly right, Chloris, for you: your daughter rather

should besiege the homes of the boys
    like a Bacchanal frenzied by the beating drum.
She is compelled by her love for
    Nothus, and carries on like a young doe in heat;

you are fit for working the wool
    shorn near famous Luceria, not for the lyre,
not for the crimson rose blossom,
    and not, old woman, for wine jars drunk to the dregs.

Danae was imprisoned by a tower of bronze
with the doors of solid oak and a ferocious
pack of watchdogs: these would have kept her quite secure
    from seducers that prowl by night,

if only Acrisius, this pentup virgin's
panicky keeper, had not made Jove and Venus
laugh out loud: for a way would be safe and open
    for a god who turned to money.

Gold enjoys going through the midst of sentinels
and forcing its way through stone: it has more power
than the lightning bolt. The house of Argos' prophet
    collapsed, for the sake of riches

sank into ruins; the man from Macedon broke
through city gates, he undermined rival rulers
with his gifts; gifts have the power to captivate
    the sternest naval commander.

The money increases, followed by worry and
greed for still more. I have been right to be fearful
of raising my head into everyone's notice,
    Maecenas, honor of knighthood.

The more a man will deny to himself, so much
the more is given by the gods: stripping myself,
I seek the camp that knows no greed, a deserter
    longing to leave the wealthy side,

a more glorious master of things I reject
than if I were said to have buried in my barns
harvests from all the plowed fields of Apulia,
    and had no good of all my goods.

A brook with clear water, a few wooded acres,
and confidence in my crops: a happier life
than fertile Africa's glittering governor
    was given—not that he knows it.

Although no Calabrian bees bring me honey,
and no wine is becoming more mellow for me
in Formian jars, and no fleeces of mine
    grow full in the pastures of Gaul,

still poverty stays away, with all its troubles,
and if I wanted more, you would not refuse it.
As my desire for things is lessened, I stretch my
    little income even further

than if I were to join Alyattes' kingdom
to the plains of Phrygia. For men who seek much,
much is never there; a man is well off when god's
    frugal hand gives him just enough.

Aelius, descended from ancient Lamus,
after whom, so they say, the Lamiae of
    earlier times were named, and the whole
        tribal line in the genealogies,

you derive your birth from that founding father
who is said to have been the first to rule the
    walls of Formiae, and the Liris
        where it spreads out over Marica's shores,

a spacious kingdom. Tomorrow her forest
will be strewn with many leaves and her shoreline
    with useless seaweed, in a storm from
        the East, if the long-lived crow is not wrong

who prophesies rain. While you can, make a pile
of dry branches; tomorrow you will treat your
    soul to strong wine and a suckling pig,
        and your household slaves will have a day off.

III · 18

Faunus, lover of the swiftly running Nymphs,
step lightly across my bounds and over my
sunlit farm, and take your leave with a blessing
    for the small weanlings,

if at the year's end a young kid is offered,
and the mixing bowl, partner of Venus, has
its plenty of wine, and the ancient altar
    smokes with much incense.

The whole flock frolics on the grassy meadow
when the fifth of December returns for you;
the joyful villagers at ease in the fields
    with resting oxen;

the lambs have no fear of the wolf strolling through;
the forests scatter their wild branches for you;
and the plowman gladly in tripletime dance
    beats the ground he hates.

How long between Inachus' reign
    and Codrus, who did not fear death for his country,
you talk of this, and Aeacus'
    family tree, and wars fought by Troy's sacred walls;

what price should we pay for a jar
    of Chian wine, with whose fire should water be warmed,
whose house is free, and at what hour
    I am rid of Samnium's cold: no word from you.

Here's to—hurry up—the new moon,
    here's to midnight, and here, my boy, 's to Murena
as augur: three parts or nine
    of wine mixed in your cups, whichever you'd rather.

The lover of the odd Muses
    begs a mixture of three times three for an inspired
poet; to touch more than three
    is forbidden for fear of a brawl, by the Grace

who holds her naked sisters' hands.
    It pleases me to go mad: why pause in blowing
on the Berecyntian flute?
    Why keep the pipes and the lyre hanging there silent?

The hands that give begrudgingly,
    I hate them: scatter the roses: let envious
Lycus hear our crazy riot
    and the girl who lives near, not right for old Lycus.

It is you, sleek and curly-haired,
    you, Telephus, lovely as the star of evening,
ripening Rhode is after;
    I burn with lingering love for my Glycera.

III · 20

Can't you see, Pyrrhus, the peril in fooling
with the cubs of an African lioness?
A bit later you will run from rough fighting,
    fainthearted robber,

when she breaks through the enclosing lines of boys
to bring incomparable Nearchus back:
a mighty duel, will the prize come to you,
    or is he for her?

In the meantime, as you draw out your swiftest
arrows, and she sharpens her terrible teeth,
rumor has it that the judge of this contest
    spurned the palm with his

bare foot, and takes his ease with a gentle breeze
in the scented curls that cover his shoulders,
handsome as Nireus was or the boy Jove
    snatched from Ida's streams.

Born with myself when Manlius was consul,
whether you promise complaining or laughter,
    or quarrels and uncontrolled passion,
        or, trustworthy wine jar, easy sleeping,

for whatever purpose the Massic was put in
your keeping, to be served on a proper day,
    come down, for Corvinus has ordered
        a mellower wine to be brought for him.

He will not, although he is soaked in the words
of Socrates, look down on you, soberly:
    they tell us that even old Cato's
        manhood was often aglow with strong wine.

You apply to a mind that is dull most times
the pleasure of your rack; you unlock the thoughts
    and secret plans of a clever man
        by the power of joy-giving Bacchus;

you restore the hopes of minds that are troubled,
and bring power and courage to the poor man:
    after you, not a shiver for crowned
        heads and their anger, nor for soldiers' swords.

Bacchus, and Venus, if she will be so kind,
and the Graces who like to stay together,
    and burning lamps will prolong your life
        till Phoebus' return drives the stars away.

III · 22

Holy Maiden, keeper of mountain and forest,
Virgin, to whom young women in labor
pray, who hear and save them from death,
    triple goddess,

bless this pine that overhangs my villa,
and each year I will gladly offer it
the blood of a boar just learning to sideswipe,
    a young boar's blood.

If you lift your upturned hands towards heaven
when the moon is new, my farm-bred Phidyle,
    if you offer the Lares incense
        and the early grain and a suckling pig,

the vines will stay fruitful, untouched by Southwind's
sickness, and the fields by the blight that makes them
    barren, and the young of the flocks by
        the dangerous season when fruits are ripe.

For the chosen victim, who grazes on snow-topped
Mount Algidus among oaks and ilexes,
    or is growing fat on the grass of
        Mount Alban, will stain the high priests' axes

with its blood. It is not proper for you to make
a large slaughter of full-grown animals:
    garland the small statues of the gods
        with crowns of crisp myrtle and rosemary.

If the altar is touched by hands that are free,
that do not flatter with costly offerings,
    the coldness of Penates will melt
        for the sacred grain mixed with crackling salt.

III · 24

More wealthy than the unplundered
    Arabian treasures and Indian riches,
you can shovel your rubble in
    throughout the land and the sea that is free to all,

but if dreadful Necessity
    hammer her adamantine nails in your tallest
rooftop, you will not be able
    to free your soul from fear, nor your neck from death's
    noose.

The Scythians, plainsmen whose carts
    carry, as is their custom, their wandering homes,
have a better life, and so do
    the stern Getae, whose acres, never divided,

bring forth everyone's fruit and grain,
    and whose law is no more than a year at farming,
then the man whose work is finished
    is replaced by another, on the same basis.

There, women spare their stepchildren,
    doing no harm to those who have lost their mother,
and no wife rules her husband with
    her dowry, and gives herself to a sleek lover.

Their large dowry is their parents'
    honor, and chastity, firm in its vow, staying
away from another's husband,
    and belief that such sin is foul, with death its price.

O whoever desires to end
    murder's desecrations and our mad civil wars,
and wishes "Father of Cities"
    inscribed on his statues, he must have the courage

to bridle our untamed freedom,
    and win a later fame, for—ah god, how sinful—
we envy and hate the living
    virtue, complain when it is taken from our sight.

What is the use of sad complaints
    if crime is not weeded out by retribution?
What can empty laws accomplish
    without moral standards? When no part of the world,

not that barred in by the blazing
    heat, nor the countries that border the farthest North,
their ground frozen over with snow,
    keeps the trader away, when the clever sailors

overcome the roughest ocean,
    and when poverty, that great disgrace, commands us
to do or suffer anything,
    and abandons the difficult path of virtue.

Let us bring to the Capitol,
    with the cheers and applause of an approving crowd,
or toss into the nearest sea
    the jewels and gems and unprofitable gold,

the cause of our greatest evil,
    if we really wish to be sorry for our sins.
The seeds of vicious avarice
    must be rooted up, and our far too delicate

characters must be molded by
 sterner training. The freeborn boy has not been taught
how to keep his seat on a horse,
 and is afraid to hunt; he knows more about games,

if you care to see the Greek hoop,
 or prefer the dice that the laws have forbidden,
and meanwhile his father, breaking
 his oaths, defrauds his business partner and his friends,

and busily hoards up money
 for a worthless heir. His dishonest wealth, of course,
keeps growing, yet there is always
 something missing: his fortune is never complete.

All yours, Bacchus, where do you bring
    me? To what groves or what grottoes am I driven,
swift with a new spirit? In what
    caverns will my thoughts be heard, setting the deathless

honor of glorious Caesar
    among the stars and in the company of Jove?
I will celebrate a noble
    new doing, still unsung by other lips. Just as

a sleepless Maenad stands awestruck
    on a hilltop, staring at Hebrus and the glare
of Thracian snow and Rhodope,
    alien country, so it thrills me to wander

and wonder at riverbanks and
    forests where no one dwells. O ruler of Naiads,
and of Bacchantes strong enough
    to uproot with bare hands the towering ash trees,

nothing minor or plain in style,
    nothing mortal will I sing. The danger is dear,
lord of wine: I follow the god,
    and my forehead is garlanded with fresh vine leaves.

Not long ago I kept in shape for the girls
and performed in battle with no little glory;
    now my weapons and my lyre, discharged
        from the service, will be held by this niche

in the wall that shelters the left side of sea—
born Venus' statue. Here, here, lay down the bright
    torches, and the levers and axes
        threatening war upon reluctant doors.

O goddess who rules over blessed Cyprus
and Memphis that never knows Thracian snows,
    O queen of love, lift up your whip and
        let arrogant Chloe have just one flick.

To evil men may these omens be given:
screeching owl and pregnant dog, or gray she-wolf,
running down from Lanuvian fields, and fox
    swollen with young ones;

and may the journey, once started, be stopped by
a snake crossing the road like an arrow,
scaring the horses. For the one I care for,
    I will be prophet,

I will awaken with prayer the talking
raven: he will come from the east too early
to return to the standing ponds and predict
    threatening showers.

May you be happy, whatever land you choose;
live long, Galatea, and remember me;
stray crow or pecker, come not from the left to
    stop you from going.

But see the commotion stirred up by setting
Orion. I know what the Adriatic
gulf is like when it's black, how the Northwester
    harms, even when clear.

May our enemies' women and children feel
the sudden rush of the rising Southwind, the
roaring of the darkened waters, and the shores
    quivering with shock.

This was how Europa consigned her body,
white as snow, to the tricky bull: the deep sea
teeming with monsters, the dangers around her,
    made the bold girl pale.

Just now in the meadows, busy with flowers,
she fashioned a garland to offer the Nymphs,
and now she can see in the glimmering night
    only stars and waves.

As soon as she came to Crete, mighty with its
hundred cities: "O father, I abandoned
my name of daughter and my duties," she cried,
    "madness possessed me.

Where have I come from? where am I? One death is
little for a virgin's guilt. Am I awake,
weeping for wrong that was done, or free of sin,
    mocked by a phantom

emptily floating through the ivory gate
bringing a dream? Was it better to voyage
across the long ocean, or to gather the
    blossoming flowers?

If anyone gave me that evil young bull now,
my anger would drive me to slash him with steel
and to break the horns from the monster I once
    loved with such passion.

I had no shame: I left the gods of my home.
I have no shame: I keep Death waiting. O gods,
if one of you hears this, I long to wander
    naked through lions.

Before these lovely cheeks are seized by ugly
starvation, and strength ebbs from the delicate
victim, while I have beauty, I ask to be
    food for the tigers.

'Sinful Europa,' pleads my absent father,
'why delay your dying? Here is an ashtree:
you luckily still have your sash: hang till your
    neck has been broken.

Or if the cliffs and the points of their deadly
rocks attract you, come, consign yourself to the
rapid winds: or would you, with your royal blood,
    rather be winding

wool for your lady, a concubine subject
to a cruel mistress?' " As she lamented,
there was Venus, with her fickle smile, and her
    boy, his bow relaxed.

Soon, when she had enough of the game, "An end,"
she said, "to anger and hotblooded quarrel,
for the bull whom you hate will surrender his
    horns for your slashing.

Wife of mighty Jove, and you do not know it.
Stop this sobbing, learn to accept with good will
this great destiny; part of the world will be
    carrying your name."

What else should I do on the feast
    of Neptune? Bring out, and quickly, the Caecuban
that I've kept in hiding, Lyde,
    and on with the siege of the castle of prudence.

The afternoon is running down,
    you see it, and as if the flying day stayed fixed,
delay invading the storeroom
    for the waiting jar dating from Bibulus' time.

We will sing in turn, beginning
    with Neptune and the green hair of his Nereids:
you reply on the curving lyre
    with Latona and swiftfoot Cynthia's arrows:

the song's finale, she who rules
    Cnidos and the gleaming Cyclades and comes to
Paphos behind her team of swans.
    Night will also be praised in appropriate song.

Descendant of Etrurian kings, a jar
of mellow wine that has never been opened,
    rose blossoms, Maecenas, and ointment
        prepared for your hair: these are at my home,

waiting a long while for you. No more delays:
don't continue to take a distant view of
    Tibur's streams, Aefula's sloping fields,
        the hills of parricide Telegonus.

Get away from disgusting luxury, and
your mountainous mansion that touches tall clouds;
    put aside the fascination of
        blessed Rome, her smoke and glamour and noise.

Very often the wealthy enjoy a change,
and plain suppers beneath a poor man's small roof,
    without tapestries and purple cloths,
        have been known to smooth a worried forehead.

Now the bright star of Andromeda's father
shows his hidden fire, now Procyon blazes
    and the star of the raging Lion
        as the sun brings back the season of drought;

now the sleepy shepherd and his weary flock
seek the shade and the brook and the thickets of
    hairy Silvanus, and the straying
        breezes have left the quiet riverside.

You are concerned with the state and its proper
condition, and fear for the city, worried
    by plots in the Far East and Bactra,
        where Cyrus ruled, and Scythian unrest.

Wisely god buries in night and its darkness
what will be the result of the days to come,
    and he laughs if men are more afraid
        than they need be. Keep this in mind: be calm,

and put in order the things at hand; all else
is carried as if by a river, that now
    flows quietly down its mid-channel
        into Etruria's sea, now tumbles

stones worn smooth, uprooted tree trunks, flock and homes,
all jumbled up, and the same uproar is loud
    in the neighboring hills and forests
        as the wild deluge infuriates streams

that once were placid. A man will live happy,
his own master, when at the close of each day
    he can say, "I have lived. Tomorrow
        the Father may fill the heavens with clouds

or with clear sunlight; but never will he turn
the things that are past to nothing again, nor
    change the pattern and take to pieces
        the gift of a single swift-running hour.

Fortune is happy in her cruel affairs
and persists in playing her arrogant games,
    changing inconstant honors about,
        kind now to me, and now to another.

While she stays, I praise her; if she rustles swift
wings, I mark down as lost what she gave, and I
     wrap my manhood about me and court
         faithful Poverty who has no dowry.

It is not for me, as the masts are moaning
in blasts from the south, to go running to my
     wretched prayers, bargaining with vows
         so my goods from Cyprus and Tyre may not

be added to the wealth of the hungry sea.
At such a time, kept safe in my two-oared boat,
     I am carried through Aegean storms
         by the winds, Pollux, and his twin brother."

My memorial is done: it will outlast bronze,
it is taller than the Pyramids' royal mounds,
and no rain and corrosion, no raging Northwind
can tear it down, nor the innumerable years
in succession, and the transitory ages.
I will not wholly die: the greater part of me
shall escape the goddess of death: I will grow on,
kept alive by posterity's praise. As long as
high priest and silent virgin climb the Capitol,
I will be known where the wild Aufidus thunders,
in the land where water is scarce, whose farmers
Daunus once ruled, a man who rose from poverty,
who led the way, adapting Aeolian song
to Italian verses. Accept the high honors
I have won by your kindness, and graciously crown
my hair, Melpomene, with Apollo's laurel.

INTRODUCTION TO BOOK FOUR AND "HYMN FOR THE CENTENNIAL"

The fourth book of lyrics was published about 13 B.C., five years before Horace's death. Some fanciful explanations have been given of this last phase of his work in lyric: that discouragement over the reception of Books I–III caused him to turn away from the form, that the assignment to write the *Carmen saeculare* ("Hymn for the Centennial") in 17 B.C. revived his energies as a lyric poet.

There may be some truth in such conjectures, but there is little evidence. That the *carmina* were not an immediate success we know from *Epistles* i. 19, where Horace refuses to stoop to luring an audience. But he is not the type of poet who writes to please the market; he had the approval of the readers who mattered to him, and that would have been enough. The simplest explanation is the obvious one: the last poem of Book III shows that he felt his lyric work was completed; he must have believed that this vein was exhausted and that he had achieved all he could with the difficult forms he had introduced to Latin poetry. It was natural for him to turn back to the conversation-poem that he had used in the *Satires* and to refine it and explore its possibilities still further in the *Epistles* (Book I was published about 20, Book II about 14 B.C.). The first Epistle tells us more of Horace's feeling: he has had enough of lyrics; he wishes to work in a looser form and to meditate on truth, without the intense "game-playing" of lyric.

It is usually suggested that Book IV was published because

of the wishes of Augustus, and this seems likely. Certainly Horace is the "official poet" in these lyrics to a degree that was not true in the first three books. The second poem takes the typical Horatian gambit of turning a refusal to write heroic poetry into a polished lyric and gives us a fine tribute to Pindar and a modest self-appraisal, but odes 4 and 14 are Pindarizing celebrations of the victories of Augustus' stepsons. They are well enough in their way, but we may find the last poem in the book, appropriately a tribute to the Augustan peace, more in the true Horatian vein.

It is notable that Maecenas makes only one appearance in this book, in ode 11. A conspiracy against Augustus in 23 B.C. involved Licinius Murena, the half-brother of Maecenas' wife, Terentia, and Maecenas allowed the news of its discovery to escape by confiding in his wife. He was no longer the trusted counselor, and we may attribute his near-absence from the lyrics to Horace's caution or tact; we should notice, however, that Maecenas is prominent in the first book of the *Epistles*, published three years after the conspiracy. That there was no breach between the poet and his friend and patron is plain enough from the tone of the reference in ode 11 and from Maecenas' request when he died, only a short time before Horace, that Augustus "remember Horatius Flaccus as you would myself."

Besides the poems that are Augustan in subject, the lyrics of this brief last volume turn to familiar themes in familiar forms, with a deepening of Horace's delicate melancholy, an awareness of impending old age. Some of them, we should remember, may well have been drafted or rejected as unsatisfactory before 23 B.C. and been worked over for this book. Others, however, bear the mark of a poet deliberately returning to an earlier theme, determined to show that he can make a fresh poem from it. Surely ode 7 is intended to recall i. 4, and a comparison points up differences as well as similarities: death is in the foreground here, as it was not in the earlier poem. The thirteenth lyric returns to a situation like i. 25 but turns from contempt to nostalgic longing and lamentation for the decay of beauty. The first ode announces the reluctance of the lyric poet and lover but proceeds with all the old Horatian charm and art: it is the poet who is *durum*, hardened by age, as the poem opens, but the loved boy who is *dure*, young and hard-hearted, as it closes.

Book IV shows us, above all, the poet who is fully assured of his position. The power of poetry had always been a favorite Horatian theme, but there is proportionally a greater preoccupation with it than in the earlier work: odes 2, 3, 6, 8, and 9 all have poetry and Horace's sense of himself as its servant and master as their central concern. In this they are close to the last *Epistles;* Horace in his final years dwells on the real love of his life, his art.

If the "Hymn for the Centennial" and Book IV produce no real surprises, no adventures into new regions of experience such as we find in the last works of Shakespeare and Yeats and Ronsard, we should not be disappointed. Whatever made Horace return to lyric after he had abandoned it, we can be thankful that he did, less for the technical skill of the more public poems than for the full mastery of the experiences Horace had made his own, in the poems already remarked and in ode 11, that happy, excited invitation to a feast, briefly shadowed by *meorum/finis amorum*, "my last love," and ending with *minuentur atrae/carmine curae*, "bitter sorrows will grow/milder with music."

IV · 1

Those wars, Venus, are long over,
    and now you provoke them again. Please, please,
      spare me.
I am not what I was when dear
    Cinara ruled me. Put an end to your efforts,

cruel mother of sweet Cupids,
    to soften the stiffness of a man now fifty
by your gentle orders: go where
    the young men invite you with flattering prayers.

This is a better time for you
    to bring, drawn by your swans' glowing wings, your
      joy to
the home of Paulus Maximus,
    if you're looking for the kind of heart to catch fire.

For he is noble and handsome,
    and speaks well in defending his troubled clients,
a young man of many talents
    who will carry the banner of your service far;

and whenever he is happy
    to have conquered the gifts of a spendthrift rival,
he will set your marble statue
    under a cedar roof, beside the Alban lakes.

There you will breathe in plentiful
    incense, and you will find delight in the music
of the Berecyntian flute
    mingled with the strings, with the pipe not forgotten;

there, twice every day, the boys
    and delicate virgins will chant the praises of
your divinity, their white feet
    beating the ground in tripletime Salian dance.

As for me, not woman nor boy
    nor the hope that believes its feelings are returned
pleases me now, nor drinking bouts,
    nor having fresh flowers wound about my forehead.

But why, ah Ligurinus, why
    does a tear now and then run trickling down my cheek?
Why does my tongue, once eloquent,
    fall, as I'm talking, into ungracious silence?

At night I see you in my dreams,
    now caught, and I hold you, now I follow as you
run away, over the grassy
    Field of Mars, over flowing streams, with your hard
      heart.

Whoever labors to be Pindar's equal,
Iulus, mounts on wings that are fastened with wax,
Daedalus-fashion, and will give his name to
    glittering water.

As a river roars down a mountain, swollen
by showers of rain, spilling over its banks,
so Pindar rages and the deep of his voice
    pours ever onward,

worthy of the laurel sacred to Apollo,
whether he is tumbling freshly minted words
through frenzied hymns, carried along on meters
    free and unruly,

whether he is chanting of gods, and kings, off-
spring of gods, who struck the Centaurs down,
a death they deserved, struck down the fire-breathing
    frightful Chimaera,

or is singing of those the palm of Elis
brings home as immortals, boxer or horseman,
and is giving them an honor finer than
    hundreds of statues,

or else is lamenting a young man, taken
from his weeping bride, exalting his manhood
and courage and golden virtues to the stars,
    envying dark Death.

Strong is the wind that lofts the swan of Dirce,
as often, Antonius, as he aims for
the cloudy heights. My methods are those of a
    bee on Matinus,

working hard to gather the sweet-tasting thyme
all about the many groves and the banks of
Tibur's streams, a painstaking minor poet,
    shaping my lyrics.

You are a bard in the grand manner: you will
celebrate Caesar, wearing the garland he
won, leading in triumph up the sacred hill
    savage Sygambri;

the Fates and the kind gods have given the world
nothing that is greater or better than he,
nor ever shall, not even if time returned
    to the golden age.

You will celebrate festivals and public
games for the answer to the city's prayers,
brave Augustus' return, and no lawsuits
    heard in the Forum.

Then, if something I sing deserves hearing, my
best voice will join in, and "O glorious
sun, worthy of praise," I will gladly chant for
    Caesar's homecoming.

As you lead the way, "Hail, God of Triumph,"
we shall sing more than once, "Hail, God of Triumph,"
all the citizens, and to the kind gods shall
    offer our incense.

Your promise is fulfilled with ten bulls and cows,
mine with a tender calf, no longer beside
his mother, growing big on rich grasses to
    satisfy my vow,

with a forehead that mirrors the crescent light
of a new moon on the third night it rises,
white as snow wherever he has a marking,
    otherwise tawny.

IV · 3

Once you have turned, Melpomene,
    your kind eyes on a man in the hour of his birth,
no training for Isthmian games
    gains him fame as a boxer, and no eager horse

will bring his Grecian chariot
    in with a winner, nor will action in wartime
decorate him with laurel leaves,
    a commander who tamed pompous threatening kings,

highlighted at the Capitol;
    but the streams that are flowing by fertile Tibur
and the crowded leaves of its groves
    form him: he will be known for Aeolian song.

Rome is the first of all cities,
    and her children believe I deserve a place in
the delightful choir of poets:
    less often now am I gnawed at by envious teeth.

O goddess of Pieria
    who control the sweet music of the golden lyre,
O you who could give, if you wished,
    the song of the swan to even voiceless fishes,

all of this is a gift from you,
    that people passing by point a finger at me
as master of the Roman lyre:
    power and pleasure, when I give pleasure, are yours.

As the eagle, bearer of the thunderbolts,
who was given by Jupiter, king of gods,
     rule over roving birds, for he proved
        true in the fair-haired Ganymede affair,

is driven by youth and natural vigor
to leave the nest, knowing nothing of struggle,
     and soon, for storms are over, the winds
        of spring have frightened but taught him to use

his untried powers, next with sudden assault
he descends, an enemy, on the sheep pens,
     and now desire for food and fighting
        thrusts him against the serpents, who strike back;

or as a lion, just weaned from the rich milk
of his tawny mother, is suddenly seen
     by a young doe, who was eager for
        good grazing and will die by his young teeth:

so Drusus, warring beneath the Raetian
Alps, was seen by the Vindelici (the source
     of whose custom that has been carried
        through all ages, arming their right hands with

Amazonian axes, I have not tried
to learn, nor can one know all things), but the mobs,
     conquerors so long and so widely,
        were conquered by a young man's strategy,

feeling the strength of a mind and a spirit
properly nourished in a favored household,
the strength of Augustus' fatherly
affection for the children of Nero.

Brave sons are begotten by brave and good men;
there in young bulls, there in horses, is the worth
of their fathers, and the ferocious
eagles do not beget pacifist doves.

But teaching develops natural powers,
and a training in goodness strengthens the heart;
when a code of ethics was missing,
faults have disfigured born nobility.

What you owe, O Rome, to the house of Nero,
witness the Metaurus River, and conquered
Hasdrubal, and that glorious day
when darkness was driven from Latium,

the first smiling day of blessed victory
since the grim African rode through the cities
of Italy, like flame through pine trees
or East wind over Sicilian waves.

After that, their efforts always rewarded,
young Roman troops grew stronger, and in temples,
ruined by the ungodly riot
of Carthaginians, gods stood once more.

And at last the treacherous Hannibal said:
"We are like deer, the prey of ravenous wolves,
pursuing them willingly, when to
trick and escape them is a great triumph.

This race, still strong after Ilium's burning,
bringing through the beating of Etruscan waves
    its holy images and children
        and elders to Ausonian cities,

like an oak on fertile dark-leaved Algidus
that was stripped by heavy double-edged axes,
    through losses, through slaughter, it derives
        its power and life from the steel itself.

Not hydra grew stronger, its body cut up,
against Hercules, who could not stand defeat,
    nor was a greater wonder brought forth
        by Colchis or Echionian Thebes.

Drown it deep, it emerges more glorious;
wrestle with it, great is its fame when it throws
    the unmarked man who thought he had won,
        and it fights battles the wives will talk of.

Now I shall dispatch no more proud messengers
to the Carthaginians: destroyed, destroyed,
    all the hope and the luck of our name
        since the total defeat of Hasdrubal."

Nothing Claudian power shall not achieve,
protected by Jupiter's favorable
    wishes, and with prudent strategy
        steered safely through the crises of war.

Born with the blessing of the gods, best guardian
of Romulus' people, you have been gone too long;
return, for you gave the city fathers' sacred
    council your word to return soon.

Return with light, blessed leader, for your homeland;
for when, like the springtime, your face has smiled upon
your people, the day goes more delightfully by
    and the sun shines still more brightly.

As a mother tries with vows and omens and prayers
to call back her boy, far away from his dear home,
lingering, over a year now, across the wide
    waves of the Carpathian sea,

delayed by the Southwind and its spiteful tempests,
and she will not turn her face from the curving shore,
so the homeland, transfixed with loyal devotion,
    is longing for Caesar's presence.

For then the cow wanders safely through its pastures,
Ceres and kind Fertility nourish the fields,
the sailors speed over seas that are quieted,
    honor takes care to be blameless,

the home is chaste, not polluted by lechery,
custom and law have wiped out the stains of evil,
mothers are praised, their children look like their husbands,
    punishment closes in on crime.

Who fears the Parthians, the frigid Scythians,
the swarms that issue from barbarous Germany,
as long as Caesar is safe and sound? Who worries
    over the war in savage Spain?

Every man spends the day on his own hillside
marrying his vines to the trees that are single,
then goes happily home to his wine, in due course
    petitioning you as a god;

with many prayers, pouring pure wine from libation bowls,
he gives you honor and joins your divinity
to the gods of his household, as Greece remembered
    Castor and mighty Hercules.

"O blessed leader, promise the long festival
the Western world desires": so we pray with dry lips
as day begins, so we pray with lips wet with wine
    when the sun sinks in the ocean.

IV · 6

God whose force was felt by Niobe's children,
punishing her boasting, and by that rapist
Tityos, and, with tall Troy nearly his, by
    Phthian Achilles,

a greater man than others, no match for you,
although he was the son of seaborn Thetis,
and, as he fought with his terrible spear, shook
    Ilium's towers.

He was like a pine tree struck by biting steel,
or a cypress toppled by an Eastern gale
as he collapsed, sprawling, and his neck was bowed
    in the dust of Troy.

He would not have hidden in the horse, the false
gift to Minerva, nor have tricked the Trojans
into rash celebration, with Priam's court
    joyfully dancing,

but openly cruel to the conquered, he
would have burned with Greek fire—ah god, the horror—
babies who could not speak, even the child
    in the mother's womb,

if your voice and that of sweet Venus had not
won over the father of gods, who agreed
to Aeneas' fate, city walls raised under
    favoring omens.

Teacher of the lute to skillful Thalia,
Phoebus, who bathe your hair in Xanthus' river,
maintain the honor of the Daunian Muse,
    smooth-cheeked Apollo.

To Phoebus I owe my power, to Phoebus
the art of song and the title of poet.
Maidens of noble birth, and boys, the sons of
    glorious fathers,

guarded by Diana, goddess of Delos,
whose bow brings down lynxes and stags as they flee,
keep strict time to the Sapphic meter and the
    beat of my finger

in the rites of chanting to Latona's son,
the rites of the moon as her light increases,
blessing the harvest, hurrying on the swift
    months in their turning.

A little later, when married, you will say:
"I performed at the sacred centennial
the hymn the gods loved, trained in the meters of
    Horace the poet."

Snow has run off, now the grass returns to the meadows
    and the leaves to the branches;
earth is passing through her round and the rivers are lower
    flowing within their banks;

with the Nymphs and her sisters the Grace takes her chances
    naked to lead her dancers.
"No hope of eternal delight," say the year and the hour as
    they
        hurry the sweet day away.

Wind from the west and the cold relaxes, then spring
    surrenders to
        summer, whose ruin must come with
plentiful autumn's prodigal harvest, and back again
    to the stiffness of winter.

Swift is the moon in its changes, but loss in the sky is
    restored;
        we, when the journey is over
down to devoted Aeneas and splendid Tullus and Ancus,
    we are dust and a shadow.

Who can say if the gods will add to our present sum
    tomorrow's bonus of hours?
Keep all you can from your sticky-fingered heir by giving
    now to your precious self.

Once you are dead, Torquatus, and solemn Minos pronounces
    final verdict upon you,
not your noble name nor skillful tongue nor honor
    brings you back to life;

chaste Hippolytus stayed in the darkness below, Diana
    did not deliver him,
and when chains of Lethe held his dearest Pirithous,
    Theseus could not break them.

I would give freely to my friends, Censorinus,
libation bowls and bronzes that took their fancy,
I would give them tripods, the prizes of Grecian
heroes, and you would not take away the poorest
gift, if only, of course, I owned many works of art
such as Parrhasius or Scopas created,
the latter in stone, the first in flowing colors,
cleverly capturing here a man, there a god.
But this is beyond me, and your rank and spirit
have no need of that kind of luxury item.
You delight in lyrics: lyrics are in our power
to give, and we are able to value such gifts.
Not public inscriptions on statues of marble
bringing breath and life back to honored generals
after death, not the swift retreat of Hannibal
when his threats were thrown back and turned upon himself,
not the flaming ruin of ungodly Carthage
proclaim the glory of the man who brought back
the riches of its name from conquered Africa
more brightly than the Muses of Calabria,
and if paper never spoke of your finest deeds,
you would lack what you deserve. Where would the son of
Mars and Ilia be, if envious silence
had stood in the way of Romulus' just reward?
The power and favor and voice of great poets
save Aeacus from the river Styx, and give him
a holy place in the islands of the blessed.

The Muse forbids a praiseworthy man to perish.
Heaven is the Muse's blessing. So courageous
Hercules shares, as he hoped, in the feasts of Jove,
and the bright constellation, Tyndareus' sons,
rescues battered ships from the depths of the ocean,
and Bacchus, with fresh vine leaves about his forehead,
brings the prayers of men to a happy ending.

Never believe the words perhaps will perish,
I, who was born near far-sounding Aufidus,
 chant for the strings' accompaniment
   by an art not commonly known before.

Though the first place is held by Maeonian
Homer, the Muses of Pindar and Ceos,
 of threatening Alcaeus and stern
   Stesichorus, have not been forgotten;

nor has time wiped out what Anacreon once
tossed off; the Aeolian girl and her love
 still breathe, and her passions are alive,
   entrusted to the music of the lyre.

Spartan Helen was not the only woman
who ever caught fire, dazzled by a lover's
 wavy hair and his gold-tinseled robes
   and his royal manner and retinue,

nor was Teucer the first to shoot an arrow
from a Cretan bow: more than one Ilium
 suffered a siege; nor has Sthenelus
   or mighty Idomeneus alone

fought battles the Muses should sing of; nor were
bold Hector and brave Deiphobus the first
 to have felt the brunt of heavy blows
   defending their chaste wives and their children.

Many a great hero was living before
Agamemnon, but they all, unlamented
    and unknown, are smothered by night that
        never ends: they have no sacred poet.

Little distinguishes buried cowardice
from hidden courage. I will not leave your name
    unspoken, not honored by my verse,
        nor allow, Lollius, all you have done

to be eaten away by oblivion's
unhindered envy. You have a character
    experienced in worldly matters,
        undisturbed by success or reversal,

swift to punish greedy fraud, and refraining
from money that attracts all things to itself,
    a consul, not for one year alone,
        but as often as you, a good, honest

judge, put your honor before your advantage,
refuse the gifts of the guilty with a look
    of scorn, clear your way with such weapons
        through the opposing crowd, a conqueror.

Not the man who possesses many things may
be truly called blessed; more truly the name
    of blessèd belongs to the man who
        knows how to use what the gods have given

wisely, and to suffer poverty's strictness,
who is more afraid of dishonor than death,
    a man who is not afraid to die
        defending his dear friends or his homeland.

O you are still cruel, still ruling by the blessings of Venus,
but when the soft down shall grow suddenly over your
   arrogance,
and the curls that now ripple about your shoulders have been
   cut off,
and the color that now is fresher than the blossom of a rose
has faded, Ligurinus, and your face has turned coarse and
   bristling:
"Ah," you will cry, as often as you see your change in the
   mirror
"the way that I feel today, why was I not like that as a boy,
   or why will my cheeks not return unchanged when I feel in
   this mood?"

IV · 11

I have a jar that is filled with Alban wine,
more than nine years in aging; in my garden,
Phyllis, there is parsley for weaving garlands;
    plenty of ivy

to tie back your hair so your beauty will shine;
the house winks with silver; the altar is wreathed
with sacred leaves, longing to be sprinkled with
    blood from a victim;

the slaves are all in a hurry; here and there
serving boys and girls go scurrying about;
the flames are leaping, tossing waves of black smoke
    up to the ceiling.

But you must be told to what celebration
you are invited: we must honor the Ides,
the day dividing April in half, the month
    of seaborn Venus,

a day that is properly sacred to me,
almost more holy than the day I was born,
for by its light my Maecenas measures the
    flowing of his years.

Telephus, the boy you want, is above you,
and he is already taken by a girl,
rich and lecherous, who keeps him fast in her
    lovable fetters.

The frying of Phaethon should warn off the hope
that wants too much, and a stern lesson is taught
by winged Pegasus who threw Bellerophon,
      his earthborn rider,

always to do what becomes you: do not hope
for more than is right, knowing that a lover
who is not your equal is wrong. Come now, my
      love, and my last love,

for after this I shall warm to no other
woman, and allow me to teach you lyrics
for your lovely voice: bitter sorrows will grow
      milder with music.

Now the breezes from Thrace, the companions of spring,
have pacified the sea and are filling the sails;
now the fields are not hard, nor the rivers roaring,
  ، swollen with the snows of winter.

She is building her nest, mourning Itys sadly,
the unfortunate swallow, forever a shame
to the house of Cecrops, her revenge too cruel
    for the savage passions of kings.

They are singing as they lie on the yielding grass
keeping their fattening sheep and playing their pipes
and delighting the god who is fond of the dark
    Arcadian hills and their flocks.

The time of the year has made us thirsty, Vergil,
but if you are longing for a drink of wine pressed
at Cales, you servant of noble young patrons,
      you must pay for your wine with nard.

Nard in a small box of onyx coaxes a jar
from its cubbyhole in Sulpicius' storehouse,
brimming with the gift of new hopes and with power
    to wash bitter worries away.

If you want these joys in a hurry, come quickly
with your merchandise: should you arrive with no gift,
I have no intention of drenching you with winecups
    like a lord whose house is well stuffed.

Really, put delay and desire for wealth away,
and keep the dark fires of death in mind: while you may,
mix a bit of silliness into your scheming:
  sometimes it's good to be foolish.

They listened, Lyce, to my prayers, the gods did,
the gods listened, Lyce: you are showing your age,
    yet you try to look pretty,
        you play around and you drink hard,

and when soused, you attempt to wake sluggish Cupid
with a shaky song. He stands alert for the lovely
    face of blossoming Chia
        who knows how to sing to the lyre.

For he flies in disgust by the withered-up oak
trees, and he hurries away from you because teeth
    turned yellow, because wrinkles
        and snow-white hair make you ugly.

Robes of Coan purple and expensive jewels
will never bring your day again, once and for all
    sealed in the public records,
        shut fast by time in its flying.

Where is Venus, ah, where is your beauty? Where is
that grace of movement? What remains of her, of her
    who once seemed to breathe with love,
        who stole me away from myself,

and was joyful, with Cinara gone, and famous
for lovely face and charming manner? The Fates gave
    a few years to Cinara,
        preserving Lyce a long time,

so her days would equal those of the ancient crow,
and the hotblooded boys could come and have a look,
    not without plenty of laughs,
        at a fire crumpled to ashes.

IV · 14

What concern city fathers and citizens
shall show, Augustus, for your merits, the full
　　roll of your honors, immortalized
　　　　by inscriptions and official records

for all ages, O greatest of princes in any
land where people are living under the sun,
　　whose strength in war the Vindelici,
　　　　with no experience of Latin rule,

have recently learned. For yours were the soldiers
with whom brave Drusus, paying them back double,
　　overthrew the Genauni, a tribe
　　　　that does not give in, and the swift Breuni

and their forts posted on the terrible Alps.
His elder brother soon joined the decisive
　　battle and, under favorable
　　　　auspices, beat the barbaric Raeti,

a marvellous sight in the midst of battle
as his carnage discouraged so many whose
　　hearts were set on the deaths of free men,
　　　　much like the Southwind when it is churning

the untamed waves, as the dancing Pleiads are
breaking through clouds, eager to disrupt the ranks
　　of the enemy, and to send his
　　　　snorting horse into the heat of battle.

As bull-bodied Aufidus tosses and turns,
flowing past Daunus' kingdom Apulia,
    when he runs amuck and threatens the
        fields that are seeded with dreadful deluge,

so Claudius with a destructive assault
demolished the barbarians' armored troops,
    and mowing down front and rear, strewing
        the earth with their dead, won with few losses:

yours was the army, yours was the strategy,
yours were the gods. For, on the very day that
    humbled Alexandria opened
        harbors and deserted palace to you,

the favor of Fortune fifteen years later
offered you a happy ending to the war,
    granting praise and the honor they sought
        to those who acted under your command.

You are a wonder to the Cantabrian,
unconquered before, to Mede and Indian,
    to the Scythian nomad, O sure
        defense of Italy and Rome our queen.

Your voice is heard by the Nile, that hides the source
of its waters, the Hister, the swift Tigris,
    by the Ocean swarming with monsters
        that bellows about the far-off Britons,

the land of Gaul, that does not shiver at death,
by the country of stubborn Iberia;
    Sygambri, delighting in slaughter,
        have put down their weapons, and bow to you.

Phoebus, as I was about to celebrate
battles and cities conquered, twanged on the lyre,
 warning me not to hoist a small sail
  on the Tuscan sea. Your era, Caesar,

has brought plentiful harvests back to the fields,
and restored to our shrine of Jove the banners
 torn from the high and mighty poles
  of the Parthians, and closed Janus' temple,

for no war was on, and imposed restrictions
on the freedom that wandered beyond proper
 boundaries, and expelled wrongdoing,
  and recalled the ancestral way of life

by which the Latin name and the power of
Italy grew, and the fame of the empire
 and its majesty stretched from the sun's
  western bed to the place of his rising.

While the state is in Caesar's charge, no civil
madness, no disturbance shall drive away peace,
 nor shall hatred, that forges its swords
  and transforms poor towns into enemies.

Nor shall those who drink the Danube's deep waters
break the Julian laws, nor shall the Getae,
 the Seres, the faithless Parthians,
  nor those born near the river Tanais.

All of us, on working days and holy days,
among the gifts of laughter-loving Bacchus,
    accompanied by wives and children,
        will first, as is proper, pray to the gods,

then, in the way of our fathers, to the sound
of Lydian flutes we will hymn our heroes
    and their noble achievements and Troy,
        Anchises, and kind Venus' descendants.

HYMN
FOR THE
CENTENNIAL

Phoebus, and Diana, ruler of forests,
the sky's bright beauty, O honored gods, to be
honored forever, grant our prayers in this
    time of devotion,

when the words of the Sybil have commanded
a choir of chosen virgins and chaste young boys
to chant a hymn to the gods who are gladdened
    by our seven hills.

Lifegiving Sun, whose bright chariot brings forth
the day and hides it again, who are reborn
new and the same, may you see nothing greater
    than Rome, the City.

Be gracious, Ilithyia, whose concern
is the time of childbirth, protect the mothers,
or, if you wish, we shall call you Lucina
    or Genitalis.

Goddess, guide our growing young ones, and bless the
decrees of the city fathers concerning
weddings, and may the laws of marriage bring forth
    many new children,

so that ten times eleven years, the proper
cycle, may bring back singing and public games
crowded into three bright days and as many
    nights of rejoicing.

And you, the Fates, whose predictions were truthful,
may the constant order of things obey your
commands, and may you add good destinies to
    those now accomplished.

May the earth be fertile for harvests and herds
and give to Ceres her garland of wheat ears;
may the crops be nourished by Jupiter's good
    breezes and showers.

Put your weapons away, be mild and gentle,
listen to the prayers of boys, Apollo;
moon goddess, crescent queen of constellations,
    listen to virgins.

If Rome is your doing, and the Tuscan coast
was won by a company from Ilium,
survivors, told to change homes and city by
    prosperous voyage,

for whom virtuous Aeneas, unharmed in
the burning of Troy, outliving his homeland,
paved the way to freedom, and would give them more
    than they left behind:

gods, help the young to learn to do what is right,
gods, help the old to be serene and quiet,
grant to Romulus' people wealth, children, and
    every honor

And the petitions, with the blood of white bulls,
of Anchises' and Venus' bright descendant,
may they be answered: may he triumph in war,
    sparing the conquered.

Now the Mede is afraid of our men, mighty
on land and sea, and of their Roman axes;
now Scythians and Indians, once so proud,
    plead for our answer.

Now Faith and Peace and Honor and ancestral
Decency and slighted Virtue venture to
return, and blessed Plenty appears once more
    with her brimming horn.

Phoebus, the prophet, graced with his gleaming bow,
and held in reverence by the nine Muses,
who eases with his power of healing the
    exhausted body,

when he sees and blesses Palatine altars,
the Roman state and Latin prosperity
he preserves forever, through future cycles
    and better ages;

and she who rules Algidus and Aventine,
Diana, hears the prayers of the Fifteen
Guardians, and listens and is kind to the
    children's petitions.

This is the wish of Jove and of all the gods:
that is the good and certain hope we carry
home, we the chorus, trained to chant Phoebus' and
    Diana's praises.

EPODES

INTRODUCTION
TO THE EPODES

"The Epodes," writes W. Y. Sellar, "are, on the whole, the least interesting and satisfactory work of Horace."[1] While more favor has been shown to them recently, especially by Eduard Fraenkel, it is hard to disagree with Sellar's verdict in the main. Horace does little in the *Epodes* that he does not accomplish more satisfactorily elsewhere. They do, however, have an important place in his works: in them we can see most clearly the transition from a satirist to a lyric poet.

Horace's first publication was Book I of the *Sermones* (*Satires*) in 35 B.C.; Book II was to follow five years later. His creative energy in the first decade or so of writing was thus given to a *genre* that suited his temperament at that time, and that was a native Latin form ("Satire is certainly wholly our own," wrote Quintilian[2]). But Horace had studied at Athens and felt the attraction of Greek poetry, and he shared the impulse of Roman writers to adapt Greek forms for Latin literature. Under the circumstances, it was natural that he should try his hand at "the bittersweet style of iambics" (*Epistles* ii. 2).[3]

The Greek master to whom he turned was the seventh-century poet from Paros, Archilochus, and he was later to claim, somewhat excessively,

[1] *Horace and the Elegiac Poets* (Oxford, 1891), p. 130.

[2] *Institutes of Oratory* (London, 1909), trans. John Selby Watson, x. 1, 93.

[3] The translation quoted here and in the following paragraph is that of Smith Palmer Bovie (Chicago, 1959).

> I first displayed
> The iambic lines of Paros to a Latin land,
> Following the meter and tone of savage Archilochus. . . .
> [*Epistles* i. 19]

Quintilian noted that "in Horace the epode is found introduced between the iambics":[4] "epode" thus refers to the alternation of short lines with long to make up the couplet, the unit of all the poems except epode 16. By the time Horace published his collection of "iambics," about 29 B.C., he had used the form for bitter invectives, but he had also begun to use it for quite different effects. He had gone, as Fraenkel says, "a long way towards composing lyrics proper, *carmina*."[5]

It would be foolish to suppose that Horace did not work simultaneously at different forms. We should rather assume that not only the epodes but probably some of the lyrics published in 23 B.C. were composed at the same time as the satires. Once this provision has been made, we can still see the epodes as testifying to Horace's increasing impulse toward the writing of lyric, which was to absorb his energies after 30 B.C.

As he does with all his works, Horace ignores the chronology of composition in arranging his seventeen epodes. He attempts, as he did with his later lyrics, to gain the maximum effect in a collection of miscellaneous poems by exploiting contrasts and recurrences in theme and tone.

The first epode reflects the troubled political situation before Actium but uses it primarily as a background for a declaration of loyalty to Maecenas and a vow of moderation. The second expresses a longing for the pleasures of country life in

[4] *Institutes,* x. 1, 96.
[5] *Horace,* p. 65.

contrast to the city but is placed in the mouth of a usurer. The third returns to Maecenas, addressing him with mock indignation at a practical joke.

The fourth epode is the first to have the full bitterness associated with the form; the fifth is a longer poèm, an attack by means of a small dramatic scene; the sixth returns to brief invective. The seventh is also bitter, a despairing speech to Roman citizens on the follies of civil war. The eighth is a scornful attack on a lecherous old woman. After five poems with the savage tone of the epode tradition, Horace uses the ninth epode to return to his relation to Maecenas and to celebrate the victory at Actium.

The tenth epode turns once more to invective; the eleventh, a humorous confession of lovesickness, contrasts with the poem that precedes it and the violent return in epode 12 to the situation and tone of 8. Horace then presents three poems that once more depart from fierce indignation: epode 13 has a brief note of the political background to point up its praise of social pleasure; 14 returns to the love theme in making its excuses to Maecenas; 15 is the lament of a rejected lover.

The last two poems round out the collection appropriately. Epode 16 begins with a bitter picture of the political situation and then matches 2 in its longing for an idyllic country life. Epode 17 bids farewell to the Canidia of 5 by recanting the attacks in a way that drives them more firmly home: it is a satirist's satiric surrender to his subject.

The bulk of the seventeen poems are invectives, and we may look more closely at these by grouping them loosely according to their occasions, personal, social, and political. It must be remembered that animosity was characteristic of the epode as a form and that it is never easy, in such a poet as Horace, to distinguish literary exercises from personal experiences.

The poems that spring, at least fictively, from a personal offense to the poet are 3, 8, 10, and 12. Epode 3 may be briefly noted as a pleasant trifle, dexterously composed, a kind of "mock epode." Dexterity is also present in epode 10, but it suffers from a lack of sufficiently stated motive. Fraenkel may be correct in believing that Horace did not wish us to be concerned with this and that the poem is simply the result of Horace's wish "to produce a polished poetic invective reminiscent of Archilochus";[6] but the bad wishes for Mevius, vividly and gleefully detailed as they are, would have more impact if we knew more about him than his smell. Epodes 8 and 12 may be fairly dismissed in Fraenkel's words as "with all their polish, repulsive."[7] All four of these poems, based on personal grievances, have Archilochian tradition behind them: the Greek poet is said to have been promised a Theban girl as a bride and to have versified father and daughter into suicide when the promise was broken (epode 6 specifically refers to this incident).

The iambic tradition encompassed more than poems of personal revenge. In five epodes, Horace's targets are offenders against society. We are again not given enough of the situation for epode 6, an attack on a slanderer, to have much of an impact, and the poem is marred by a sudden turn near the end from the neatly developed metaphor of dogs to the presentation of the poet as a bull. Epode 14, after beginning in

[6] *Ibid.*, p. 31.

[7] *Ibid.*, p. 58.

personal resentment, gains power by putting the condemnation of the arrogant and pompous former slave in the mouths of the Roman citizens. Fraenkel presumes that Horace wrote epode 5 not to attack Canidia and witchcraft as social menaces, but because he needed a fresh and interesting victim for his iambics.[8] Whatever the truth may be, it is one of the best of the epodes, a skillful recreation of a scene of horror and pathos, and a neat patterning of the victim's plea, the witches' activities, Canidia's incantation, and the victim's curses. Epode 17, probably composed after both epode 5 and *Satires* i. 8, is clever but somewhat long-winded, with its excessive calling upon legendary precedent (though this may be a deliberate parody of a plea for mercy).

Epode 2 is both the best known of the poems and a special problem. Wilkinson remarks on the "immense popularity" of the epode in the Renaissance and later, adding that "few people would now rate this among the more remarkable of Horace's poems."[9] Fraenkel calls its spirit "very different from anything likely to be found in a work of an early iambist" and states that "if we leave for a moment the mocking conclusion, we may see in this poem a fundamentally true, if slightly idealizing, expression of Horace's own nostalgic longing for the life of the country-side. . . ."[10] But it is precisely the mocking conclusion that must be accounted for. Does it invalidate the emotion of what precedes it? The poem is best read, I believe, with an awareness that Horace is knowingly drawing on a very familiar daydream of urban societies, presenting it most sympathetically in the opening section, but

[8] *Ibid.*, p. 63.

[9] *Horace and His Lyric Poetry*, p. 165.

[10] *Horace*, p. 60.

allowing it to grow more and more distorted and sentimental-
ized, dwelling more and more on ease and luxury even in the
country as we approach the conclusion, so that by the end a
pretty vision has been muddied by a greedy personality. Cer-
tainly the poem, read properly, contrasts greatly with the lyr-
ics expressing Horace's joy in his country life; it belongs,
basically, with the poems attacking social offenders. Alfius
could never stand a week of the kind of life he describes, and
he loves the business world he supposedly loathes. There is no
reason, of course, why we should not think that Horace has
depersonalized conflicting attractions he recognized in himself
as well as others.

"The nature of the poetry of Archilochus, viewed as a whole,
demanded that . . . the life and struggles of the commonwealth
should play a part."[11] Epodes 7 and 16 are directed to sup-
posed gatherings of Roman citizens, and both contain the dis-
gust with civil upheavals that recurs throughout Horace's
lyrics. Both poems were presumably composed before the vic-
tory at Actium, perhaps before Horace became intimate with
Maecenas and the court circle. Both are poems of political de-
spair. Epode 7 begins as fierce invective, contrasting the con-
quests of the past and the possible triumphs of the present
with the actual civil conflict that is destroying the empire, but
it ends by relinquishing its attack on the guilty citizens and
accepting with weary bitterness the curse on Rome. The open-
ing of epode 16 is powerful, but the poem loses force with the
excesses of rhetoric in the citizens' vow; and the longing for
the Isles of the Blest, understandable enough, is indulged in

---

[11] Fraenkel, *Horace*, p. 47.

rather than employed for a conclusion that would match the opening in power.

In the remaining poems, Horace stays within the metrical pattern of the epode but moves away from its spirit. Epode 15 has some of the sting of the form, especially in its conclusion, but its quality comes not so much from bitterness as from the mixed feelings with which the scorned lover remembers the scene in which love was pledged and struggles to assure himself that he will really harden his heart. Epode 11 gives us not only a declaration of longing but a humorous recognition of its follies. Love plays its part also in the pleasant if trifling epode 14; the opening lines were to provide a starting point for a far greater lyric by Keats.

In contrast to the political despair of the other epodes, epodes 1 and 9 express Horace's personal and political commitments to Maecenas and Augustus. In themes, general quality of style, and in several turns of phrase they anticipate the *carmina*. And with epode 13 we have a poem that in setting, theme, and literary art belongs as much with the later lyrics as with the epodes.

These six poems give us, clearly enough, the emergence of Horace as a lyric poet. But it would be improper to suggest too wide a gap between the other eleven epodes and the *carmina*. The note struck in these early lyrics is not absent from the later work: iii. 6 has as much bitterness as any epode, but it is under finer poetic control; and even the coarsest of the epodes, 8 and 12, have their more finished counterparts in i. 25 and iv. 13.

EPODES

1

And so, dear friend, you are off with our light cruisers
    to meet their towering vessels,
and every danger to Caesar, Maecenas,
    you are ready to make your own.
What of us? if you come safely through, life for us
    is a joy: if not, a burden.
Should we do as you tell us, enjoy our leisure,
    pleasant only when you are here?
Or bear these hardships with a ready will, the right
    way for men who have not gone soft?
We will bear them, and over the peaks of the Alps
    and unwelcoming Caucasus,
or to the farthest corner of the Western world,
    stout of heart, we will follow you.
You ask how my efforts can be useful to you,
    peace-loving and weak as I am?
As your companion, I shall be less afraid;
    fear is greater in those apart,
as a mother bird is afraid of the serpents
    that may glide towards her unfledged chicks
all the more when they are alone, though she could be
    no more help if she were with them.
I will gladly enlist in this war and all wars
    in hope of winning your favor,

not of more wealth, for my plows to be dragged behind
    a longer string of yoked oxen,
or my flock to be taken, before the dog days,
    to cool Lucanian pastures,
or to have a gleaming country home in the hills
    near Tusculum's Circean walls.
Enough, more than enough have I been enriched by
    your kindness: I will not hoard wealth
to bury in the earth like Chremes the miser
    or squander like a spendthrift boy.

2

"A man is happy when, far from the business world,
    like the earliest tribe of men
he cultivates the family farm with his team,
    and is free from usury's ties
(not as a soldier, stirred by the trumpet's wild cry,
    nor quaking in an angry sea),
when he keeps away from the Forum and the proud
    doorways of influential men.
This is his life: when the shoots of his vines mature,
    he marries them to tall poplars,
or, in a secluded valley, he looks over
    his lowing cattle as they graze,
and pruning away useless branches with his hook,
    grafts more fruitful ones to the trees,
or he puts up pressed honey in his well-scrubbed jars
    or shears the struggling, helpless sheep;
above all, when through his lands Autumn lifts his head
    with a crown of ripening fruit,
how delighted he is, plucking the grafted pears
    and the purple cluster of grapes
as your offering, Priapus, and Silvanus,
    protector of boundary lines.
How pleasant to rest, sometimes beneath an old oak,
    sometimes on a carpet of grass;
all the while the brook glides by between its high banks,
    the birds are trilling in the trees,
and the splashing waters of springs play counterpoint,
    a summons to easy slumber.

But when the time of winter and thunderous Jove
      comes on with its rain and its snow,
with his pack of hounds from here, from there, he forces
      the fierce boars towards the ready nets,
or stretches a wide-meshed net on its polished pole,
      a snare for the greedy thrushes,
and the trembling rabbit and the far-flying crane
      he traps in his noose, a good catch.
Who would not forget, in such a life, the sorrows
      and cares that accompany love?
But if a chaste wife would do her part in caring
      for the home and the dear children,
like a Sabine woman or the sunburned wife of
      a strong Apulian farmer,
would pile seasoned firewood beside the sacred hearth
      for her weary husband's return,
and shutting the frisky flock in their wattled pen,
      would milk their swollen udders dry,
and bringing out this year's wine, still sweet in its cask,
      would prepare a home-cooked supper,
I could not be more pleased by Lake Lucrine oysters,
      or by turbot or by scarfish,
should winter as it roars over Eastern waters
      drive some of them near our seacoast;
no African hen or Ionian pheasant
      would make its way to my belly
more enjoyably than olives chosen from the
      ripest branches in the orchard,
or leaves of meadow-loving sorrel and mallows
      that are good for a sick body,
or a lamb slaughtered on the Feast of Boundaries,

or a kid retrieved from a wolf.
How delightful, at such a feast, to see the flock
    hurrying home from the pasture,
to see the worn-out oxen as with weary necks
    they drag along the upturned plow,
and the homebred slaves, that crowd a rich house, in place
    about the gleaming household gods."

When Alfius the usurer had said all this,
    on the brink of a country life,
he collected all of his money on the Ides,
    invested it on the Calends.

3

Whenever a man uses his ungodly hands
    to strangle his poor old father,
make him eat garlic: it's deadlier than hemlock.
    Farmers' guts must be like iron.
What kind of poison is boiling in my belly?
    Have I been tricked by a salad
with a dressing of vipers' blood? Or has that witch,
    Canidia, defiled this food?
When the handsome leader, among his Argonauts,
    attracted the eye of Medea,
she smeared Jason with this, and so he could harness
    bulls that had never felt a yoke;
this anointed her gifts, her revenge on that whore,
    and off she flew with her dragons.
Nothing's as bad, not the Dog Star's hovering heat
    over dried-out Apulia,
nor the gift on the great shoulders of Hercules
    that kindled and blazed to the bone.
But if ever again you get this evil urge,
    Maecenas, you joker, then may
your dear meet your every pucker with a slap
    and lie at the edge of the bed.

4

Like the natural enmity of wolves and lambs
    is the clash between you and me,
you, with the scars of a length of rope on your back
    and of harsh fetters on your shins.
For all that you strut about, proud of your money,
    Luck won't change your family tree.
Can't you see, as you parade up the Sacred Way
    in your full three yards of toga,
how the faces of those who are walking past you
    take on a look of pure loathing?
"This ex-slave, lashed by the whips of the magistrates
    till he tired the town crier,
cultivates a thousand Falernian acres,
    his ponies wear out the Appian,
and he, with a nobleman's air, takes a front-row seat,
    shrugging off the law of Otho.
What good will it do to send out so many ships,
    heavy cruisers with splendid prows,
against the bands of pirates and runaway slaves,
    when this, this is what's in command?"

5

"But by all of the gods in heaven, the rulers
    of the earth and the human race,
what is the meaning of this noise and the wild way
    all of you are looking at me?
In the name of your children, if your pains were real
    and Lucina heard and helped you,
by this useless luckcharm I wear on my toga,
    in Jove's name, whom you will displease,
I beg you: why look at me like a stepmother
    or a beast cornered with a spear?"
After wailing this in a shaky voice, the boy
    stood there, stripped of his childish things,
his body only half grown: it might have softened
    the hearts of ungodly Thracians.

But Canidia, whose head and disheveled hair
    were writhing with tiny vipers,
commanded that wild fig trees, uprooted from tombs,
    commanded that sad cypresses
and eggs and feathers of the night-flying screech owl,
    smeared with the blood of a foul toad,
and herbs imported from poisonously fertile
    Iberia and Iolcos,
and bones snatched from the jaws of a ravenous bitch
    be burned in the magical flames.
Meanwhile Sagana, skirts tucked up, sprinkled the house
    with water from Lake Avernus,

and her hair was wild and bristling, as if she were
    a sea-urchin or charging boar.
Veia, bothered by never a twinge of conscience,
    was digging a hole in the ground
with a hard hoe, and was groaning with the effort,
    a pit for the boy's burial,
where he would die as he stared at food that was changed
    two or three times in the long day,
his mouth above ground only as far as swimmers
    keep their chins out of the water,
and then his marrow, cut out, and his parched liver
    would be mixed in a love potion,
as soon as his eyes, fixed on the food denied him,
    had wasted away with hunger.
Naples, that city of gossips, is whispering,
    and so are all the towns nearby,
that she did not stay away, mannish, lecherous
    Folia of Ariminum,
whose Thessalian spells charm the moon and the stars
    and pluck them out of the heavens.

Then cruel Canidia with her wicked teeth
    gnawed the uncut nail of her thumb.
What did she say? what didn't she say! "O faithful
    witnesses of all my doings,
Night, and Diana, mistress of the silences
    in which secret rites are performed,
now, come help me now, turn now your wrath and power
    against those houses that hate me.
While in the dreadful forest the beasts are lying
    still in a deep and peaceful sleep,

may Subura's dogs bark at an old man playing
     lecher, with everyone laughing;
never have these hands prepared perfume more perfect
     than the one that now anoints him.
What has gone wrong? Why should the baneful mixture
     of barbaric Medea fail?
These avenged her, before she fled, on that proud whore,
     the daughter of mighty Creon,
when the robe, the present drenched in poisoned blood, took
     the new bride in a blaze of fire.
And yet I overlooked not an herb nor a root
     lurking in difficult places.
He is lying asleep on his scented mattress,
     not a thought of any mistress.
Ah! ah! he struts where he pleases: some enchantress
     more clever than I has freed him.
By means of potions, Varus, of greater power—
     O the bitter tears you shall shed!—
you shall hurry back to me; more than Marsian
     charms shall evoke your love again.
I will mix stronger drinks, I will pour stronger drinks
     to counteract your aversion,
and sooner shall the heavens sink under the sea
     and the earth be stretched above them,
before you refuse to burn with desire for me
     as pitch burns in a smoky fire."

After this, the boy tried no longer to quiet
     the ungodly with gentle words,
but unsure of what speech would best break the silence,
     he spat Thyestean curses:

"Your magic spells have no power to change right and wrong,
      nor to change human destiny.
My curses shall haunt you; no sacrificed victim
      shall avert my terrible curse.
When in the death you ordered I have breathed my last,
      I will come by night, a Fury;
as a ghost, I will rip your faces with curved claws,
      such is the power of the Dead,
and I will settle upon your uneasy breasts
      and drive away sleep with terror.
Rocks shall strike you from all sides: street by street the mob
      shall beat you to death, filthy hags.
Later the wolves and the birds of Esquiline
      shall divide your unburied flesh,
and my parents, living on when, ah! I am dead,
      shall be there to witness these things."

6

You turntail mongrel when you are up against wolves,
    why pick on innocent strangers?
Why not turn, if you dare, your empty snarls this way,
    and try me, who will bite you back?
For like a Molossian or tawny Spartan,
    dogs that are faithful to shepherds,
I will trail through heavy snow, with my ears pricked up,
    whatever wild beast is ahead;
you, when you've filled the woods with your frightening howls,
    will sniff at the food that's flung you.
Beware, beware: for against those who are evil,
    fiercely I raise my ready horns,
like the castoff son-in-law of false Lycambes
    or Bupalus' harsh enemy.
Well, if someone with poisonous teeth comes at me,
    should I quit and cry like a child?

You, the guilty, where are you running, where? why are
    your hands clutching swords they had sheathed?
Has it been too little, the Latin blood that spilled
    in a flood over fields and seas,
not for the Roman to set ablaze the haughty
    towers of envious Carthage,
nor for the Britons, still untouched by our swords, to march
    down the Sacred Way in fetters,
but to answer the Parthians' prayers, to ruin
    this city with its own right hand?
This is not the way with the wolves or the lions;
    they turn only on other beasts.
What drives us: blind madness, some inhuman power,
    perhaps guilt? Give me an answer!
They say nothing, and their faces turn sick and pale,
    and their battered feelings are numb.
This is the answer: a harsh fate haunts the Romans,
    and the evil of fratricide,
since the innocent blood of Remus stained the earth,
    a curse on all his descendants.

You, with the stink of a long lifetime, dare to ask
    who's draining my manhood away,
when your teeth are blackened and old senility
    plows its wrinkles in your forehead,
and your filthy arsehole gapes between your shrunken
    buttocks, just like a leaky cow's!
It maddens me to see your breast and withered tits
    that look like a mare's udder,
and your flabby belly and your shriveled-up thighs
    and your swollen calves below them.
Enjoy your riches, as the ancestral statues
    lead the way for your funeral,
and may no matron be seen parading after
    freighted with rounder pearls than yours.
And what of your Stoic pamphlets that art apt to
    lie under little silk pillows?
Do the illiterate really stand less stiffly
    or their rods droop any sooner?
But if you should want to get a rise out of me,
    you'd better work at it by mouth.

I rejoice with you in the triumph of Caesar,
    Maecenas. How soon shall we drink
the Caecuban put aside for celebrations
    beneath your high roof, as Jove smiles,
and the flute and the lyre join in a medley of
    Dorian and Phrygian songs?
As we did when Pompey, that son of Neptune, fled,
    driven from the sea, his ships burned,
for all that he threatened our city with the chains
    of the runaway slaves, his friends.
A Roman, ah god,—will times to come believe it?—
    a slave to a woman's orders,
bears his weapons and stakes, a soldier who can stand
    to serve under wrinkled eunuchs,
and the sun sees the shame of oriental tents
    in the midst of army banners.
One look at this, and two thousand Gauls turned their mounts
    the other way, crying "Caesar,"
and the enemy ships, commanded to sail left,
    turned sterns and hid in the harbor.
Hail, God of Triumph! Why not bring out the golden
    chariots and the unyoked bulls?
Hail, God of Triumph! No general equals him,
    not the one who fought Jugurtha,
not Africanus, whose courage raised for him
    a monument over Carthage.
Beaten by land and sea, the enemy changes
    his scarlet mantle to mourning,

and scurries towards Crete, famed for its hundred cities
    (the winds are not in his favor),
or towards the Syrtes that are tossed by the Southwind,
    or he steers an uncertain course.
Boy, bring the larger goblets over here to us
    and Chian wine, or Lesbian;
better still, keep our seasickness under control
    by pouring us some Caecuban.
It is good to shake off fears and worries for Caesar
    with the joys of carefree Bacchus.

10

The omens are black as the ship casts off and sails
    with stinking Mevius on board.
Keep your mind on your work, Southwind, batter both sides
    of the hull with the roughest waves.
May dark Eastwind scatter the ropes and broken oars
    all over the churning ocean;
may Northwind be roused, with the power that shatters
    shuddering oaks on tall mountains.
May no kind star be seen in the blackness of night
    once surly Orion has set;
may the seas he sails over be no more peaceful
    than they were for the Greek victors
when Pallas turned her anger from Troy in ashes
    onto Ajax' ungodly ship.
O what sweat is in store for the sailors with you,
    and for you, a yellowing face
and that usual effeminate wail of yours
    and prayers to indifferent Jove
when the Ionian gulf, in a roar with rain
    and Southwind, breaks your ship to bits.
And should you be stretched out on the curving seacoast,
    a plump prize, a pleasure for gulls,
then a randy goat and a lamb shall be offered
    to the gods who rule the tempest.

11

Pettius, I cannot find joy, as once I did,
in composing my little poems: love has hit me hard,
love, that longs to make me more than all the others
burn with the flame of desire for tender boys or for girls.
Three Decembers have shaken beauty from the woods
since I abandoned my mad pursuit of Inachia.
Ah, it makes me ashamed: I was in such a state:
I was the talk of the town. I regret all the banquets
where my lassitude and my silence and my sighs,
heaved from the bottom of my heart, showed that I was
in love.
"So a poor man's honest nature hasn't a chance
against riches," I would moan, pouring my grief out
to you,
when I was hot and stirred up with wine and the god
who removes inhibitions coaxed my secrets from hiding.
"If ever I let my anger loose to rage in
my heart, and scatter these worthless consolations, that
give
no relief to my cruel wound, to the four winds,
humble no more, I will not rival men not my equal."
When in your presence I had sternly praised this course
and was told to go home, I wandered with uncertain
steps
to the doorposts, O, unfriendly to me, and O
the hard threshold, that I battered with my loins and
my sides.

And now I am mastered by love for Lyciscus
    who boasts he is more tender than any little woman,
from which nothing friends say has power to free me,
    not their honest advice nor their strictest admonitions,
nothing but another flame, for a dazzling girl,
    or for a graceful young boy, who leaves his long hair
    unbound.

12

What do you want with me, woman? An elephant's more
  your type.
      Why do you send me gifts, and why these
letters? I'm not a muscular boy, and my nose isn't stuffed.
      I have one sharp sense; I can scent a
polyp or a stinking goat lurking in hairy armpits
      more keenly than hounds a sow in hiding.
What a sweat and what a rank smell rise all over her
      flabby flesh, when a penis is primed,
and she fumbles to ease her insatiable frenzy, and then her
      makeup runs, her complexion of moist
chalk and crocodile dung, and then as she reaches the peak
  of her
      spasm, she tears at the mattress and sheets.
And she attacks me for being squeamish with bitter words:
    "You are not so limp with Inachia;
three times a night for Inachia, always soft for one
      tumble with me. May Lesbia die in
torment, the bawd who procured me a sluggish bull like you,
      after I'd had Amyntas of Coos,
O the sinews of his inflexible rod were firmer than
      a young tree deeprooted in a hill.
Woolly fleeces were dipped again and again in Tyrian
      purple, and for whom? You, no one else,
so there'd be no guest your own age whose mistress
      seemed to think more of him than yours.
O, I am so unhappy: you avoid me, as a lamb fears
      savage wolves, and deer the lions."

Savage the storm that has closed in the skies, and Jove
    comes down in rain and snow: now the sea, now the
      woods
roar in the Northwind from Thrace. Let's take the chance,
  my friends,
    the day has given us, and while our legs are nimble
and the time is ripe, let's wipe age from our furrowed brows.
    You there, bring out some wine from the year I was
      born.
No talk of other things: god with a welcome change
    may put them right again. But now is the time
for the pleasures of Persian ointments, and Mercury's lyre
    to ease the heart of its weight of fears and worries,
as the famous Centaur once sang to his mighty pupil:
    "Unconquerable boy, mortal son of divine Thetis,
the country of Troy lies in wait for you, where the chilly
  waters
    of slim Scamander and smooth-gliding Simois flow,
from which the Fates, in the fixed pattern they weave, have
  cut off
    your return, and your seaborn mother shall not bring
      you home.
While you are there, ease all your misfortunes with wine and
  song,
    for unlovely sorrow the sweetest consolations."

14

Why has an easygoing slackness suffused all my senses
    with such a deep forgetfulness,
as if my feverish lips had drunk to the dregs from the bowl
    that brings on the sleep of Lethe?
You ask this so often, plainspoken Maecenas, that it hurts
me.
    For the god, the god forbids me
to reach the last page of the verses that I have begun,
    the song I have promised so long.
They say that when he burned with love for Bathyllus from
Samos,
    Anacreon was just the same,
and many a time he sang his laments to his hollow lyre
    in his plain and simple meters.
You are feeling love's heat yourself, poor man. So no lovelier
flame
    set besieged Ilium ablaze?
Be glad of your fate. Phryne, once a slave, torments me:
    she can't be content with one man.

15

It was night, and the moon was gleaming in a tranquil sky
 in the midst of the smaller stars,
when you, who would soon scorn the power of the mighty
gods,
  pledged yourself to be true to me,
your arms lingering, clinging about me more closely than ivy
 imprisons a majestic oak:
as long as the wolf should trouble the flock, and the sailor's
bane,
  Orion, the seas of winter,
and the breezes discompose the untrimmed hair of Apollo,
 so long this love of ours would last.
O Neaera, you will have your fill of grief: I'm still a man!
  For if there's manhood in Flaccus
he'll not stand for you giving yourself every night to another,
 but enraged, he'll seek a true love;
never shall his firmness give way to your hated beauty
  once his bitterness takes firm hold.
And you, whoever you are, happier than I, strutting now,
 puffed up because I am downcast,
whether you are rich, with flocks and many an acre,
  and Midas' river flows for you,
whether twiceborn Pythagoras' mysteries cannot escape you,
 and Nireus was less handsome,
ah, well, still you will lament some day that she loves another.
  But it will be my turn to laugh.

16

Now still another generation is being erased by a civil war
    and Rome's own power is bringing her to ruin,
she who was never destroyed, not by the nearby Marsians,
    nor by threatening Porsena's Etruscan troops,
nor by Capua's envious power, nor savage Spartacus,
    whom neither Gallic rebellions in times of trouble
nor the blue-eyed boys of uncivilized Germany conquered,
    nor that hatred of mothers and fathers, Hannibal:
we shall destroy her, an ungodly generation, a curse in our
    blood,
    and once more animals alone shall dwell here.
Conquering savages, ah god, shall tread on the ashes, and
    riders
    shall trample the city under their thundering hooves,
and the bones of Romulus, kept from the wind and sun,
    shall be—a scene of horror—scattered in scorn.

Possibly all, or the better part of you, wish something wiser:
    do you long to be free of these evil doings?
Then accept no other decision, but as the Phocaeans
    fled from their city, swore they would never return
to their family fields and gods, and left their shrines
    to become the homes of boars and ravenous wolves,
let us go wherever our feet shall take us, wherever
    the waves and south or strong southwest winds shall
      choose.
Does this suit you? or has someone a better proposal?
    The omens are good: why hesitate to board ship?

Swear this, however: when rocks shall rise from the ocean
    depths
        and float, our return is no longer forbidden;
nor shall it be shameful to trim our sails and make for home,
    when
        the Po shall wash the tip of Mount Matinus,
or when the lofty Apennines jut out into the sea,
        and when a strange desire makes monstrous couplings,
new kinds of lust, and tigers enjoy being mounted by deer,
        and the dove shall play false with the hawk,
and the herd shall have faith in the lion and lose all fear,
        and the goat become sleek and take to salt water.
When we have sworn this, removing all hope of a sweet
    return,
        let us be on our way, all citizens,
or those above the dull-witted herd: defeatists and weaklings
        can rest in peace on their unlucky beds.

You still have manhood in you: no more of this girlish
    wailing,
        but hurry away, beyond the Etruscan coast.
Widespreading Ocean awaits us: let us seek the fields,
        the happy fields and the islands of the blest,
where the earth is not plowed, but yearly it yields the grain,
        and the vine is not trimmed, but forever flourishes,
and the branch of the olive never fails to blossom,
        and the black fig, ungrafted, adorns its own tree,
honey drips from the hollow oak, from the lofty hills
        the light-stepping spring comes splashing down.
There the goats need no orders to come to the milking pails,
        and the flock returns gladly with swelling udders,

and the bear does not growl as he circles the sheepfold at
    evening,
        and the earth does not swell up with vipers.
And we shall wonder at greater blessings: the rainy Eastwind
        does not wash away crops with a flood of showers,
and the fertile seeds are not scorched in the dried-up clods,
        for heat and cold are controlled by the king of the gods.
No diseases infect the flock, no raging heat
        from a star can dry up the herd with drought.
Never did a ship manned by Argive rowers reach here,
        nor a shameless Colchian set foot on this soil,
no Phoenician sailors swing their yardarms this way,
        nor did the long-suffering crew of Ulysses.
Jupiter set these shores apart for a god-fearing people
        when he debased the golden age with bronze;
first with bronze, then with iron he hardened the ages, from
    which
        my words show the god-fearing are granted refuge.

"Now, O now I submit to your powerful art,
and on my knees I beg, in the name of Proserpina's kingdom,
in the name of the inviolable godhead of Diana,
in the name of the books of incantations that can
unsettle the stars, and call them down from the skies,
Canidia, make an end at last of your magic spells
and unwind, unwind the circle of your whirling charm.
Telephus won the compassion of Nereus' grandson, Achilles,
the man against whom in his pride, he had marshaled the
  army
of Mysia, against whom he had hurled his sharp-pointed
  spears.
The women of Troy anointed the corpse of manslaying
  Hector
that was handed over to the dogs and the birds of prey,
after the king had left the walls of the city and fallen,
ah god! at the feet of hardhearted Achilles.
When Circe was willing, the crew of long-suffering Ulysses
divested themselves of the bristles and the tough hides
on their bodies, then the power to think and to speak
returned, and the lovely look of human faces.
I have been paid back more than enough by you,
lady most loved of seamen and door-to-door salesmen.
My youth has flown away, and my blushing cheeks
have left me; yellow skin now clings to my bones;
your magical mixtures have turned my hair white;
there is never a moment's relief from suffering,
night after day, day after night, and I cannot
draw a breath to ease the cramp in my chest.

In this state, I am forced to believe what I once denied,
that Sabine incantations can attack the heart,
and Marsian spells can give one a splitting headache.
What more do you want? O sea and earth, I'm on fire
more than Hercules was when smeared with the poisonous
blood of Nessus, more than the living Sicilian
flame of blazing Mount Etna; until I turn
to dry ashes, to be wafted off by wicked winds,
you are a sweatshop, turning out Colchic poisons.
Where does this end? What penalty will you impose?
Speak up: I promise to pay the price you demand,
I am ready to atone, whether you insist
on a hundred bulls, or wish your praises sung
to the lying lyre: chaste and impeccable,
you shall waddle among stars, a gold constellation.
Castor, outraged because of the libel on Helen,
and mighty Castor's brother, succumbing to prayer,
restored to the poet the sight they had taken away:
please—for you have the power—release me from madness:
O you were never spawned in a back alley,
you are not a hag whose rituals scatter
newly buried ashes in potter's field.
You have a kind heart, and your hands are clean,
and Pactumeius is your very own child, and it was
your own blood that stained the cloths the midwife washed,
even if you did bounce robustly out after labor."

"Why this stream of prayers to ears that are shut?
Rocks that are lashed by Neptune's high seas in winter
are not more deaf to the cries of shipwrecked sailors.
So you should go scot-free to laugh about broadcasting
Cotytian rites, the festivals of free love;

you, the lord high censor of Esquiline magic,
should get away with setting the whole town talking of me?
What a waste then, the money paid to Paelignian witches,
the time spent learning to mix a fast-acting poison!
But a doom is in store for you, longer-lasting than you will
    pray for:
you must drag out, you wretch, an unwelcome life, so that
    you
will be always on hand for a new kind of torture.
The father of faithless Pelops is longing for rest,
Tantalus, starving forever for the bountiful banquet;
Prometheus, bound to the vulture, is longing for rest;
Sisyphus is longing to settle his rock at the top
of the hill: but the laws of Jove forbid it.
You shall long sometimes to leap from tall towers,
sometimes to pierce your heart with a Noric sword,
and you shall tie, with no luck, the noose about your neck,
melancholy, sick and tired of life.
Then I will ride your hateful shoulders like a horseman,
and I will spurn the earth in my towering triumph.
Should I, who have power to make wax images feel
(as you ought to know, you spy), whose incantations
have the power to draw the moon down from heaven,
I who can summon the shades of those who are ashes
and mix the potion that arouses passion,
should I wail that on you alone my art is useless?"

NOTES

P. 25 THE ROYAL MONUMENT: The Regia, at the southeastern end of the Forum, supposedly the royal palace of Numa in former times. It was the official headquarters of the Pontifex Maximus and adjoined the Temple of Vesta.

P. 26 "FIRST ONE": *Princeps,* the title conferred on Augustus in 28 B.C.

P. 27 THE BRIGHT CONSTELLATION: Castor and Pollux.
THE FATHER OF WINDS: Aeolus.

P. 30 THE TEMPLE WALL: It was customary for those who escaped from a shipwreck to dedicate a plaque to Neptune, together with the clothes in which they had survived.

P. 32 THE SIBYL'S ECHOING GROTTO: A fountain and grotto at Tibur were sacred to Albunea, a nymph and prophetess.

P. 34 THE SON OF SEABORN THETIS: Achilles, whose mother tried to keep him from the Trojan war by disguising him as a girl in the palace of the king of Scyros.

P. 39 LEDA'S SONS: Castor and Pollux.
THE JULIAN STAR: The fortunes of the family line of Julius Caesar and Augustus.

P. 42 SHIP: The poem is allegorical; the ship represents the state.
CINCTURE OF ROPES: Ropes were bound lengthwise about the hull to strengthen it.
NO GODS LEFT ON BOARD: Small statues of gods were usually placed in the stern for protection.

P. 43 CRETAN ARROWS: Crete was famous for its archers.

P. 44 GREATER THAN HIS FATHER: Diomed's father was Tydeus, one of the seven leaders of the army of Polynices, Oedipus' son, against Thebes.

P. 45 JUPITER HIMSELF: Here, as elsewhere, the origin of Jupiter as sky-god must be recalled.

AN ENEMY ARMY: Literally, an arrogant army, an enemy plow. The epithets are reversed in an attempt to capture some of the force of the Latin word-order, in which the sentence ends with *insolens*, "arrogant."

P. 47   THE STINKING HUSBAND'S HAREM: The she-goats.

P. 51   FILLED THE THEATER . . . : Maecenas was seriously ill in 30 B.C., and was applauded when he entered the theater after his recovery.

P. 57   WHAT NORTHERN KING: Probably the Dacian, Cotiso, who menaced the northern border of the empire in 30 B.C.

P. 59   I. 28: This poem is something of a problem; some editors have believed it is really two poems, the second beginning at line 21. It may be read somewhat satisfactorily as the monologue of a dead sailor, washed up near the tomb of Archytas.
THE FATHER OF PELOPS: Tantalus.

P. 60   THREE HANDFULS: Enough earth for formal burial, without which the soul could not cross the river Styx.

P. 67   JOINING NAILS; WEDGES . . . : Symbols of power, all tools of construction.
WRAPPED IN WHITE CLOTH: The priests of Fides sacrificed to her with the right hand, the source of loyalty, protected by white cloth.

P. 69   THE TOGAS OF MANHOOD: On March 17, boys of sixteen were invested with the *toga virilis*.
RED-LETTER DAY: Literally, a day marked with white chalk, signifying good luck.

P. 70   NOW IS THE TIME: Augustus took Alexandria in 30 B.C., and Antony and Cleopatra committed suicide.

P. 72   EXPENSIVE GARLANDS: Literally, garlands sewn on linden bark. These were professionally made by sewing flowers to the inner bark of the linden tree, whereas myrtle garlands were homemade.

P. 74 JUNO AND OTHER GODS: Juno was the patroness of Carthage, which was obliterated in 146 B.C.

P. 75 CARTHAGINIANS IN BOTH: There were Carthaginian settlements in Spain and Libya.

P. 78 ATREUS' SON: Agamemnon. The captured girl is Priam's daughter, Cassandra.

P. 80 THE SHEEP WHO WEAR SKINS: They were covered with skins to protect their wool.

P. 81 WHO HAS RESTORED YOU: Augustus in 29 B.C. permitted those who had served against him to return to Italy.

P. 87 WARMONGERS OVERSEAS: Literally, the warlike Cantabrians and the Scythians, separated from the Romans by the barrier of the Adriatic.
THE LATEST STYLE: Literally, bound in a knot, like a Spartan girl's hair.

P. 88 THE SEA OF SICILY: Sea-battles with Carthage were won at Mylae (260 B.C.) and off the Aegates Islands (242 B.C.) in the First Punic War, giving Rome control of Sicily.
GIANT SONS OF EARTH: Monstrous creatures who attacked the gods. They were protected by Earth, their mother, from the gods, but were defeated by Hercules, a mortal who aided the Olympians.

P. 94 DISDAIN THE SOD: As material for the roof of a house, or a simple altar.

P. 95 A CONSUL'S LICTOR: One of the duties of this attendant was to order a crowd to disperse.

P. 97 THE PROTECTION OF JOVE: In astrology, Jupiter is a favorable planet, Saturn a malignant one. The reference is to Maecenas' recovery from illness, as in i. 20.

P. 98 MERCURY'S POETS: Mercury invented the lyre.

P. 99 EXTENDING THE SHORE: It was fashionable in the Augustan Age to build a home on piles of masonry jutting out from the shore.

P. 100 THE SERVANT OF DEATH: Charon. The legend referred to is unknown.

TANTALUS' DESCENDANTS: Pelops, Atreus, Agamemnon.

P. 101 EUHOE: The cry of the worshipers of Bacchus.

ROD OF POWER: The thyrsus, a staff wound with ivy and tipped with a pine cone. Its touch could bring one under the god's power, and fertilize the land.

YOUR BLESSÈD BRIDE: Ariadne, whose crown was made by Vulcan and became a constellation.

P. 102 WHEN CERBERUS SAW YOU: Bacchus went to the underworld to bring back his mother, Semele. The horn is probably a drinking-horn.

P. 104 THE FIELD OF MARS: The Campus Martius, where the assembly was held for the election of magistrates.

SICILIAN BANQUETS: Damocles, who had flattered Dionysus I of Syracuse in Sicily, was given a banquet where a sword was suspended over his head by a single hair to teach him the "joy" of wealth and power.

P. 106 TAKE OR LEAVE THE AXES: The symbols of authority carried by the lictors before the magistrates.

P. 107 THE SECRET RITES OF CERES: The Eleusinian mysteries, revealed only to initiates, who were forbidden to reveal them. They originated in the cult at Eleusis in Greece and were later adopted by the Romans.

P. 108 POLLUX AND ROAMING HERCULES: Mortals who earned deification.

P. 109 MY HATED GRANDSON: Mars was the son of Juno; the priestess of Troy was Ilia, Romulus' mother.

P. 112 THE BROTHERS: Otus and Ephialtes attempted to reach heaven by placing Mount Ossa on Olympus, and Pelion on Ossa, but were struck by Jove's lightning. In the following lines Horace blends several mythical attacks on the Olympians into one.

P. 114 THE SACRED SHIELDS: In the reign of Numa, a shield supposedly fell from heaven, and eleven others were modeled after it to guard it from theft. The shields were intrusted to the Salii.

P. 119 THE MAD STAR: Capra, the goat, rose in the evening at the beginning of October, the time of the autumnal storms.

P. 121 MARCH THE FIRST: The Matronalia, when married women sacrificed to Juno.
WAR WITH EACH OTHER: The struggle for Parthia between Tiridates and Phraates, 31–27 B.C.

P. 125 YOU HAVE POWER . . . : The allusions are to Orpheus playing the lyre.

P. 129 RETURNING FROM SPAIN: Augustus returned to Rome in 24 B.C., after almost three years in Gaul and Spain. He had been seriously ill in Spain, and there were rumors of his death. The comparison to Hercules alludes to the hero's seizure of Geryon's cattle in Spain.
HIS WIFE: Livia.
THE SISTER: Octavia, Antony's widow.

P. 132 THE HOUSE OF ARGOS' PROPHET: Amphiarus foresaw that the attack of the Seven against Thebes would fail, but his wife, Eriphyle, bribed by a gold necklace, persuaded him to join the army. He was killed in battle; she was killed by their son, who in turn was driven mad by Furies.

THE MAN FROM MACEDON: Philip, the father of Alexander the Great.

P. 135 THE FIFTH OF DECEMBER: The country feast-day of Faunus.

P. 138 THE BOY JOVE SNATCHED: Ganymede.

P. 139 III. 21: The poem is adressed to Diana, "triple goddess" because she ruled, under different names, the moon, the earth, and the underworld.

P. 147 THE TALKING RAVEN: The croaking of the raven and his return to the pool were thought to be signs of rain.
COME NOT FROM THE LEFT: The unlucky side.

P. 150 THE FEAST OF NEPTUNE: July 23.

P. 151 ANDROMEDA'S FATHER: Cepheus, who became a constellation.
PROCYON: The smaller Dog Star, which precedes the greater, Sirius, in its rising.
THE STAR OF THE RAGING LION: Regulus, which rises at the end of July.

P. 160 PINDAR: Of all the kinds of lyric Horace attributes to Pindar, only the odes celebrating athletic triumphs have survived.

P. 161 AUGUSTUS' RETURN: Augustus was away 16–13 B.C., attending to threats to Gaul by German tribes.
NO LAWSUITS HEARD: On a day of celebration, the courts did not hear pleas.

P. 164 AMAZONIAN AXES: Two-edged.

P. 165 THE CHILDREN OF NERO: Tiberius and Drusus, Augustus' stepsons.
THE GRIM AFRICAN: Hannibal.

P. 166 A GREATER WONDER: The allusion is to the legends of warriors springing up after Jason at Colchis and Cadmus at Thebes sowed dragon's teeth.

P. 167 IV. 5: The occasion for the poem is Augustus' absence referred to in IV. 2.

P. 169 IV. 6: A poem occasioned by the festival of 17 B.C., for which Horace composed the "Hymn for the Centennial."

P. 173 THE MAN WHO BROUGHT BACK: Publius Cornelius Scipio Africanus Major (236–183 B.C.). He was celebrated in the poetry of the Calabrian poet Ennius.

P. 180 SHE IS BUILDING: The allusion is to the legend in which Procne, daughter of the king of Athens, killed her son Itys and fed the flesh to her husband, Tereus, who had raped her sister Philomela. She was changed into a swallow, Philomela into a nightingale.
SULPICIUS' STOREHOUSE: Storehouses on the Tiber, built by Sulpicius Galba.

P. 184 HIS ELDER BROTHER: Tiberius.

P. 185 THE VERY DAY: August 29, 30 B.C.

P. 186 CLOSED JANUS' TEMPLE: The arch of Janus, at the north end of the Forum, closed in time of peace.
THE JULIAN LAWS: The treaty conditions imposed by Augustus, whose adopted family line was Julius.

P. 188 HYMN FOR THE CENTENNIAL: In 249 B.C., during the First Punic War, sacrifices and festival games were held in the Campus Martius. A century later, during the Third Punic War, the festival was held again. There was no celebration in 49 B.C., but in 17 B.C. Augustus used the tradition for a religious festival celebrating the success of his rule. (He gained from the keepers of the Sibylline books a justification for the date on the basis of the Etruscan interpretation of a *saeculum* as 110 years.) The original festival had honored the gods of the underworld; Augustus' festival honored Apollo, whose devotion he encouraged, and Diana.

Horace was assigned to write the *Carmen saeculare,* the official hymn, which was performed by two choruses, with 27 boys in one, 27 girls in the other, on June 3, the last day of the festival.

THE DECREES OF THE CITY FATHERS: Augustus, in 18 B.C., issued an edict approved by the Senate designed to reward the fathers of large families and to penalize unmarried men and childless married couples.

P. 190 THE FIFTEEN GUARDIANS: The *quindecimviri,* keepers of the sacred books of the Sibyl. They had charge of the festival.

P. 200 LIGHT CRUISERS: Liburnians, light, fast, easily maneuvered ships, used by Augustus' fleet against the higher and heavier ships of the Egyptian navy in the battle of Actium (31 B.C.).

P. 203 THE FEAST OF BOUNDARIES: February 23.

P. 206 THE TOWN CRIER: The *praeco,* who called out the offense over and over as a slave was being whipped.

THE LAW OF OTHO: Lucius Roscius Otho, a tribune, sponsored a law passed in 67 B.C. that set aside the first fourteen rows in the theater for freeborn Romans of equestrian rank.

THE BANDS OF PIRATES: The fleet of Sextus Pompeius, son of Pompey the Great, who held the waters about Italy from 42 B.C. until his defeat by Agrippa in 36 B.C.

P. 213 THE ANCESTRAL STATUES: Wax figures of the distinguished ancestors of the deceased, carried before the corpse in funeral processions.

P. 214 THE TRIUMPH OF CAESAR: At Actium, 31 B.C.

THAT SON OF NEPTUNE: Sextus Pompeius took the title of "son of Neptune" after his victories over Augustus' fleet.

WEAPONS AND STAKES: The stakes were used to construct barricades.

TWO THOUSAND GAULS: Cavalry which had fought with Antony, but deserted to Augustus before Actium.

THE ENEMY SHIPS: The reference is rather uncertain, but it can be noted that at Actium Cleopatra's fleet fled, and Antony's followed.

THE GOLDEN CHARIOTS: The general honored for a triumph rode in a chariot decorated with gold; bulls that had never been yoked for plowing were part of the procession and were sacrificed at the temple of Jupiter.

P. 220 THE FAMOUS CENTAUR: Chiron, the teacher of Achilles.

P. 225 NO DISEASES. . . : The arrangement of the last ten lines is a matter of editorial dispute. I have used lines 61–62 in the Loeb edition as lines 57–58 in the translation, an order that seems more logical.

MANNED BY ARGIVE ROWERS: The crew of the Argo; Medea is the "shameless Colchian."

P. 226 YOUR WHIRLING CHARM: The bull-roarer, a board whirled at the end of a stick, used in casting spells; the spell could be broken by reversing the movement.

P. 227 RESTORED TO THE POET: The Greek poet Stesichorus (630–555 B.C.), who had written satirically of Helen and was said to have been blinded until he wrote a poem of recantation.

YOUR VERY OWN CHILD: Apparently Canidia had stolen a baby and pretended to bear it herself.

GLOSSARY

The reader should note that, while Horace's lyrics are highly allusive, most of them are clear enough to be understood and enjoyed at a first reading, without checking every allusion. This glossary is intended to clarify some otherwise obscure passages, satisfy curiosity, and indicate the range of the poet's geographical, historical, and mythological references, and of his acquaintances among his contemporaries.

I have assumed that the most familiar classical myths and the larger geographical areas need no gloss.

A considerable number of the persons in the poems—e.g., Lyde, Cinara, Postumus, Thaliarchus—are addressed pseudonymously or are fictitious.

ACHAEMENES. Grandfather of Cyrus the Great, and founder of the Persian royal family.

ACHERON. A river in Hades; Hades itself.

ACHERONTIA. A small town in Apulia, on Mt. Vultur.

ACRISIUS. In legend, the father of Danae, who shut her in a brazen tower because of a prophecy that her son would kill him. Zeus came to her as a shower of gold; their son, Perseus, accidentally killed Acrisius with a discus.

AEACUS. A legendary king, grandfather of Achilles; after his death, he was made one of the judges in Hades.

AEFULA. A town in the hills of Latium.

AELIUS. *See* Lamia.

AEOLIAN. The Aeolians were one of the Greek races. They settled Lesbos; Sappho and Alcaeus, the lyric poets, wrote in the Aeolian dialect.

AFRICANUS. In epode 9, Scipio Africanus Minor (185–129 B.C.), who destroyed Carthage in 146 B.C.

AGRIPPA, Marcus Vipsanius (63–12 B.C.). A close friend and counselor of Augustus who commanded the fleet that defeated the pirates of Sextus Pompeius in 36 B.C.

AJAX. In i. 15, and epode 10, Ajax son of Oileus, as distinguished from Ajax son of Telamon. The former raped Cassandra in the temple of Pallas Athene during the taking of Troy and was punished by being shipwrecked on the voyage home.

ALBAN. A mountain in Latium.

ALBIUS. In i. 33, probably Albius Tibullus (60–19 B.C.), the elegiac poet to whom Horace also addresses *Epistles* i. 4.

ALCIDUS. A mountain about 20 miles east of Rome.

ALYATTES. In the sixth century B.C., the ruler of the wealthy Lydian empire, in Asia Minor, and the father of Croesus.

AMPHION. Legendary king of Thebes, supposed to have raised the city walls by playing the lyre.

ANACREON. A Greek lyric poet of the sixth century B.C., who avoided the complex lyric forms of Alcaeus and Sappho.

ANCHISES. A prince of Troy, loved by Venus. Aeneas was their son.

ANCUS. One of the legendary first kings of Rome.

ANIO. A river, tributary to the Tiber, that flows near the town of Tibur.

ANTILOCHUS. In the *Iliad*, the son of Nestor, killed in battle by Memnon.

ANTIOCHUS. King of Syria, defeated by Rome in 190 B.C.

ANTIUM. A town on the coast of Latium, with two temples dedicated to the goddess Fortuna.

APPIAN WAY. A busy road leading south from Rome.

APULIA. A district in southeastern Italy, on the Adriatic Sea, where Horace was born.

ARCHYTAS (*ca.* 400–365 B.C.). A Greek general, philosopher, and mathematician, from the town of Tarentum, said to have invented the screw and the pulley.

ARCTURUS. The star whose setting, at the end of October, ushered in the autumnal storms.

ARIMINUM. A town in Umbria, in northeastern Italy.

ATLAS. A Titan, father of Maia, who was the mother of Mercury, by Jove.

ATREUS. Father of Agamemnon and Menelaus. He killed his brother Thyestes' sons and served their flesh to their father at a banquet, bringing a curse on himself and his children.

ATTALUS III. King of Pergamus, in Asia Minor, who left his kingdom and wealth to the Roman people in 133 B.C.

AUFIDUS. A river in Apulia, near the birthplace of Horace.

AULON. A region near the town of Tarentum.

AUSONIAN. The Ausonians were early inhabitants of central and southern Italy.

AVENTINE. The southernmost of the seven hills of Rome, on which a temple of Diana was situated.

BACTRA. A city in eastern Parthia.

BAIAE. A resort town on the Bay of Naples.

BANDUSIA. A fountain near Venusia, where Horace was born. The spring of iii. 13 is the one on Horace's farm to which he transferred the name.

BANTIA. A town in Apulia, near Venusia.

BASSAREUS. A name given to Bacchus, referring to the fox-skins worn by his worshipers.

BELLEROPHON. The legendary hero who rode the winged horse Pegasus and killed the Chimaera; he was thrown by Pegasus when he tried to ride up to heaven.

BERECYNTIAN. Berecyntus is a mountain in Phrygia, in Asia Minor, where the rites of the goddess Cybele were celebrated.

BIBULUS. Consul in 59 B.C. The name means "fond of drinking."

BISTONIAN. The Bistonians were a tribe in Thrace.

BITHYNIA. A country in northern Asia Minor, on the Black Sea.

BREUNI. A tribe in the Tyrol.

BUPALUS. A Greek sculptor of the sixth century B.C., attacked in verse after he made an unflattering statue of the poet Hipponax.

CAECUBAN. Wine from Caecubum, in southern Latium.

CAESAR. In Horace's lyrics, the name usually refers to Augustus (C. Julius Caesar Octavianus). In i. 2, the name refers in the last line to Augustus, earlier to Julius Caesar.

CALABRIA. A district that was the heel of the boot that is Italy.

CALENDS. The first day of the month.

CALES. A town in Campania, south of Latium. Calenian wine comes from here.

CALLIOPE. The Muse of epic poetry, but referred to in a less restricted sense in iii. 4.

CAMILLUS, Marcus Furius. Military and political leader of the fourth century B.C., who defeated invading Gauls.

CANTABRIA. A territory in northern Spain. Its people were defeated in 29 B.C. but not subdued until 19 B.C.

CAPITOL. The southwest peak of the Capitoline Hill in Rome, on which the temple of Jupiter Optimus Maximus was situated.

CAPUA. The chief city of Campania, south of Latium, which joined Hannibal aganist Rome in 216 B.C., but was defeated in 211 B.C.

CASTALIA. A spring on Mt. Parnassus, sacred to the Muses and Apollo.

CASTOR. Twin brother of Pollux, son of Leda, brother of Helen. He was deified and worshiped as a guardian of seamen.

CATILUS. With his brothers, Tiburtus and Coras, he came from Arcadia and founded the town of Tibur.

CATO, Marcus Porcius. The elder Cato (235–147 B.C.) was famous for his integrity, asceticism, and his attempts to reform Roman morals. The younger Cato (95–46 B.C.) was leader of the republicans after Pompey's death and committed suicide after Julius Caesar's victory.

CE' ROPS. The legendary first king of Attica and founder of Athens.

CENSORINUS, Gaius Marcius. Consul in 8 B.C.

CEOS. An island in the Aegean Sea, birthplace of the poet Simonides (*fl.* 500 B.C.).

CHIAN. Wine from the island of Chios, in the Aegean Sea.

CHIMAERA. A legendary monster with the head of a lion, the body of a goat, and the tail of a serpent, killed by Bellerophon when he rode the winged horse Pegasus.

CHREMES. A stock name for an old miser in comedy.

CLIO. The Muse of history.

CNIDOS. A town in Caria, in southern Asia Minor, an important center for the worship of Venus.

COAN. From the island of Cos, in the Aegean Sea.

COCYTOS. The "stream of lamentation" in Hades.

CODRUS. A king of Athens who gave up his life when a prophecy foretold that the Dorian invaders would take the city if the king did not die.

COLCHIS. A country on the eastern shore of the Black Sea, from which Medea, the king's daughter and a sorceress, fled with Jason and the Golden Fleece.

CONCANI. A tribe in Spain.

CORVINUS, Marcus Valerius Mersala. A student with Horace in Athens who served under Brutus and Antony and later joined Augustus; consul in 31 B.C., a commander at Actium, and a friend of the poet Tibullus.

COTISO. A Dacian leader defeated in 29 B.C.

COTYTIAN. Cotytto was a goddess worshiped originally in Thrace.

CRAGUS. A mountain in Lycia, in Asia Minor, the home of Latona, mother of Apollo and Diana.

CRASSUS, Marcus Licinius. Triumvir in 60 B.C. with Pompey and Caesar. He was defeated and killed by the Parthians in 53 B.C., and thousands of his soldiers surrendered and settled among the Parthians.

CRISPUS, Gaius Sallustius (d. A.D. 20). Grandnephew and adopted son of the historian Sallust.

CURIÚS, Manius. Consul in 290, 275, and 274 B.C.; he defeated Pyrrhus and the Samnites, and retired to his farm, rejecting any share of the plunder.

CYBELE. An Asiatic goddess, whose cult was introduced to Rome in 204 B.C. Processions of her priests were allowed in Rome in Horace's time, but citizens were forbidden to take part in the rites, which were accompanied by frenzied music and dancing.

CYCLADES. A group of islands in the southern part of the Aegean Sea.

CYNTHIA. Diana. Mt. Cynthus was in Delos, the island where she was born.

CYPRUS. The island in the eastern Mediterranean where Venus is supposed to have come after she rose from the sea.

CYRUS. Founder of the Persian Empire in the sixth century B.C. The Parthian kings of Horace's time claimed descent from him.

DACIA. A territory north of the lower Danube, added to the Roman Empire in A.D. 106.

DANAUS. The legendary founder of Argos, who fled with his fifty daughters from his brother Aegyptus. The latter's fifty sons pursued them, and Danaus was forced to consent to their marriage with his daughters. He ordered the girls to kill their husbands on their wedding-night, and all but one (see iii. 11) did. Their punishment in Hades was to try forever to fill with water jars that had holes in the bottom.

DAUNUS. A legendary king of Apulia:

DEIPHOBUS. A Trojan warrior, brother of Hector.

DELLIUS. ii. 3 is probably addressed to Quintus Dellius, who changed sides several times during the civil war, but joined Augustus in 31 B.C., and became his close friend.

DELOS. An island in the Aegean Sea, birthplace of Apollo and Diana.

DIRCE. A fountain near Thebes, the birthplace of Pindar.

DORIAN. The Dorians were a tribe that settled in Greece in the twelfth century B.C. "Dorian" songs are martial, as contrasted in epode 9 to the lighter Phrygian music.

DRUSUS, Nero Claudius (38–9 B.C.). Son of Tiberius Claudius Nero and Livia, stepson of Augustus, younger brother of Tiberius.

ECHION. One of the warriors who grew from the dragon's teeth sown by Cadmus at Thebes. He married Cadmus' daughter.

ELIS. A territory in Greece containing the town of Olympia, where the games were held.

ENCELADUS. One of the giants who attacked Jove. He was buried beneath Mt. Etna.

EPIRUS. A district of Greece on the Ionian Sea.

ERYMANTHUS. A mountain in Arcadia.

ERYX. A mountain in Sicily, on which Aeneas is supposed to have dedicated a temple to Venus.

ESQUILINE. One of Rome's seven hills, on which a paupers' cemetery was situated.

ETRURIA. The district north of Latium, on the west coast of Italy, where the Etruscans lived in early times.

ETRUSCAN. The Etruscans were early inhabitants of northwestern Italy. The Etruscan bank (i. 2) of the Tiber is the right bank.

EUTERPE. The Muse of flute-playing.

FABRICIUS, Gaius. Heroic and incorruptible in the war against Pyrrhus (281–275 B.C.).

FALERNUS. The country at the foot of Mt. Massicus in Campania, south of Latium, noted for its wine.

FAUNUS. An Italian god of forests and fields, identified after Greek influence with Pan.

FORENTUM. A town in Apulia, south of Venusia.

FORMIAE. A town on the coast of Latium, noted for its wine.

FUSCUS, Aristius. A poet and grammarian, who makes an appearance in *Satires* i. 9.

GALAESUS. A river in southern Italy, near Tarentum.

GARGANUS. A mountain near the Adriatic, in eastern Apulia.

GELONI. A Scythian tribe.

GENAUNI. A tribe in the Tyrol.

GERYON. A legendary three-bodied giant, killed by Hercules.

GETAE. A Thracian tribe, north of the Danube.

GROSPHUS, Pompeius. A Roman aristocrat who owned Sicilian estates. He is mentioned in *Epistles* i. 12.

GYAS. One of the giants who attacked the Olympian gods.

HAEDUS. The two stars whose rising, at the beginning of October, was a prelude to the autumnal storms.

HAEMUS. A mountain in Thrace.

HEBRUS. The principal river of Thrace.

HELICON. A mountain in Boeotia, sacred to Apollo and the Muses.

HISTER. The lower part of the Danube, flowing through Dacia.

HYLAEUS. One of the Centaurs in the fight with the Lapithae.

HYMETTUS. A mountain near Athens.

HYPERBOREANS. A mythical people of the far North, who lived in a kind of earthly paradise.

IBERIA. In iv. 5, Spain; in epode 5, a district in Asia Minor.

ICAROS. An island in the Aegean Sea.

ICCIUS. A friend of Horace who enlisted in the Roman expedition against Arabia (25 B.C.), and who is addressed in *Epistles* i. 12.

IDA. A mountain in Phrygia.

IDES. The middle day of the month, the fifteenth day of March, May, July, and October, the thirteenth of the other months.

IDOMENEUS. In the *Iliad*, a Cretan warrior who fought on the Greek side.

ILIA. The mother of Romulus and Remus, thrown into the Tiber and married by the river-god. In i. 2, Julius Caesar is thought of as her descendant, his assassination was therefore an injury to her, and the Tiber rises to avenge his wife.

ILITHYIA. A Greek goddess of childbirth, identified in the Centennial Hymn with Diana, and with Lucina (usually Juno as goddess of childbirth), and Genitalis, a title invented by Horace, presumably to clarify the allusion.

INACHUS. The legendary first king of Argos.

INDUS. A river in India.

IOLCOS. A town in Thessaly.

IONIA. A section of the west coast of Asia Minor. Ionic dances were wild and wanton.

ISTHMIAN. Athletic contests were held every five years at the Isthmus of Corinth.

IULUS, Antonius. Mark Antony's son, stepson of Octavia, Augustus' sister.

JUGURTHA. King of Numidia, defeated and captured by Gaius Marius, executed at Rome in 104 B.C.

LACEDAEMON. Sparta.

LACONIA. The Greek country whose capital was Sparta.

LAMIA, Lucius Aelius. A young friend of Horace, consul in A.D. 3, died in A.D. 33. In iii. 17, the Lamiae are the cannibal Laestrygonians of the *Odyssey*.

LANUVIUM. A town in Latium, about 20 miles from Rome.

LAOMEDON. A legendary king of Troy who refused the promised payment to Neptune and Apollo for building the city walls.

LAPITHAE. A mountain people in Thessaly who fought with the drunken Centaurs at the wedding of Pirithous.

LARES. Italian gods of the home and fields, not distinguished in Horace's time from Penates.

LARISA. A city in Thessaly.

LATIUM. The district on the west coast of Italy where Rome is situated.

LATONA. Mother of Apollo and Diana, by Jove.

LESBOS. An island off the coast of Asia Minor, the birthplace of Alcaeus and Sappho.

LICINIUS, Lucius. Consul in 23 B.C., who conspired against Augustus and was executed. He had been adopted by Aulus Terentius Varro, and so became the brother of Maecenas' wife, Terentia.

LICYMNIA. A pseudonym for Terentia, Maecenas' wife.

LIPARA. An island north of Sicily.

LIRIS. A river in Latium.

LOLLIUS, Marcus. Consul in 21 B.C., governor of Syria in 2 B.C. His army was defeated by German tribes in 16 B.C.

LUCANIA. A district in southwestern Italy.

LUCERIA. A town in Apulia.

LUCINA. Juno as goddess of childbirth.

LUCRETILIS. A mountain in Sabinum, near Horace's farm.

LUCRINE. A lake near Naples.

LYCAEUS. A mountain in Arcadia.

LYCAMBES. A Theban who broke his promise to marry his daughter to the poet Archilochus (*fl.* 700 B.C.). Father and daughter supposedly were driven to suicide by the consequent satiric verses.

LYCIA. A country in southern Asia Minor.

LYCURGUS. A legendary king of Thrace, blinded and driven mad when he opposed Bacchus.

LYDIA. A country in central western Asia Minor.

MAECENAS, Gaius (*ca.* 70–8 B.C.). Aristocrat of Etruscan descent, counselor of Augustus, patron and friend of Horace and Vergil.

MAEONIA. A part of Lydia, in Asia Minor.

MAIA. Daughter of Atlas, mother of Mercury, by Jove.

MANLIUS, Torquatus. Consul in 65 B.C., the year Horace was born.

MARCELLUS, M. Claudius. In i. 12, the immediate reference is to Augustus' nephew and adopted son (43–23 B.C.), but it suggests also the general of the third century B.C. who captured Syracuse in the Second Punic War.

MARICA. A nymph whose sacred grove was near the mouth of the Liris.

MARSIANS. Inhabitants of a mountainous district in central Italy noted for its soldiers and its witches. The Marsian War (90–88 B.C.) was a revolt of Italian districts against Rome.

MASSIC. Wine from Mt. Massicus, in northern Campania.

MATINUS. A mountain in Apulia.

MELPOMENE. The Muse of tragedy, but sometimes spoken of by Horace as the Muse of lyric.

MEMPHIS. An Egyptian city, where there was a shrine of Venus.

MERIONES. In the *Iliad*, the charioteer of Idomeneus of Crete, an ally of the Greeks.

METAURUS. A river of Umbria, in northeastern Italy, where in 207 B.C. Hasdrubal's Carthaginian army was defeated by C. Claudius Nero.

METELLUS, Quintus Caecilius. Consul in 60 B.C., when Pompey, Caesar, and Crassus formed the first triumvirate.

MINOS. (1) Mythical king of Crete, son of Zeus; (2) one of the giants who attacked the Olympian gods.

MITYLENE. A city on the island of Lesbos.

MOLOSSIA. A district in eastern Epirus, in Greece.

MONAESES. A Parthian nobleman.

MURENA. In ii. 19, probably Lucius Licinius Murena, addressed in ii. 10.

MYCENAE. A city in the Greek district of Argos, at its peak of greatness *ca.* 1200 B.C.

MYRMIDONS. Inhabitants of Phthiotis, in Thessaly, which was ruled by Achilles.

MYRTOAN. Part of the Aegean Sea between the Peloponnese and the Cyclades.

NEREUS. A god of the sea, father of the Nereids.

NIOBE. She boasted of her superiority, because of her seven sons and seven daughters, to Latona, and her children were killed by Latona's children, Apollo and Diana.

NIPHATES. A mountain in eastern Armenia.

NIREUS. In the *Iliad*, one of the most handsome of the Greek heroes.

NORIC. Noricum was a district south of the Danube, famous for the quality of its steel.

NUMANTIA. A Spanish town, which resisted the Romans, 141–133 B.C.

NUMIDIA. A country in North Africa.

OPUS. A town in Locris, in Greece.

ORICUS. A town in Epirus, in Greece, on the Ionian Sea.

ORION. A hunter of Boeotia, a giant, of whose death various legends were told, as in iii. 4, and who became a constellation.

PACORUS. Son of Orodes, king of Parthia, who defeated a Roman army in 40 B.C.

PAELIGNIANS. An Italian tribe in Samnium, noted for witchcraft.

PALATINE. The hill on which Rome was founded and a temple of Apollo was situated.

PALINURUS. A cape on the western coast of Lucania, in southern Italy.

PANAETIUS (*ca.* 180–*ca.* 110 B.C.). A Greek Stoic philosopher who visited Rome about 150 B.C., and whose ethical treatises had a great influence on Roman thought.

PAPHOS. A town in Cyprus, the island sacred to Venus.

PAROS. An island in the Aegean Sea noted for its white marble.

PARRHASIUS (*fl.* 400 B.C.). A Greek painter.

PARTHIA. "On one frontier only did Rome confront a rival power of anything like equal stature. This was the Parthian Empire beyond the Euphrates. . . . In their own country the Parthians were deadly enemies, as Roman armies learned more than once to their cost" (Harold Mattingly, *Roman Imperial Civilisation*, p. 114). Augustus was not nearly as successful against the Parthians as Horace sometimes suggests. Several of the lyrics refer to their strategy of pretending to run away, then reversing and shooting at their pursuers.

PATARA. A city in Lycia, in Asia Minor, where there was a famous oracle of Apollo.

PAULUS, L. Aemilius. A general who died in battle at Cannae in 216 B.C.

PAULUS FABIUS MAXIMUS. Consul in 11 B.C., friend of Augustus and Ovid.

PELEUS. Legendary king of Thessaly, father of Achilles. He rejected Hippolyte, wife of Acastus, who then told her husband Peleus had attempted her. Acastus tried unsuccessfully to kill him.

PENATES. Italian gods of the home, not distinguished in Horace's time from Lares.

PENTHEUS. A legendary king of Thebes, whose palace was destroyed in an earthquake, and who was killed by his mother and sisters when he attempted to prevent the Theban women from worshiping Bacchus.

PHALANTHUS. A Spartan who founded Tarentum in 707 B.C.

PHILIPPI. A town in Macedonia, where Brutus and Cassius were defeated by Antony and Octavian.

PHOCAEA. Northernmost Ionian settlement on the coast of Asia Minor. After the triumph of Cyrus in 534 B.C., the Phocaeans migrated rather than surrender to the Persians.

PHRAATES. By murdering his father and brothers, he became ruler of Parthia in 37 B.C.

PHRYGIA. A country in eastern Asia Minor.

PHTHIA. A town in Thessaly, where Achilles was born.

PIERIA. A district in Thessaly near Mt. Olympus, the home of the nine Muses.

PINDUS. A mountain in Thessaly.

PIRITHOUS. A legendary king of the Lapithae, who attempted to carry Proserpina from Hades. He was a close friend of Theseus.

PLANCUS, Lucius Munatius. Governor of Gaul in 43 B.C., consul in 42. Deserted Antony for Augustus before the battle of Actium.

POLLIO, Gaius Asinius (76 B.C.–A.D. 5). Consul in 40 B.C., founder of the first Roman public library, author of tragedies and of a history of the civil wars (none of which have survived), subject of Vergil's fourth and eighth eclogues. In 39 B.C., he was given a triumph for his victory over the Parthini, a tribe in Dalmatia, on the east coast of the Adriatic Sea.

POLLUX. Twin brother of Castor, son of Leda, brother of Helen, worshiped as a deity of seamen.

POLYHYMNIA. The Muse of sacred song.

POMPEIUS. In ii. 7, not identified.

POMPILIUS, Numa. Legendary king of Rome after Romulus.

PONTUS. A district in Asia Minor, on the Black Sea.

PORPHYRION. One of the giants who attacked the Olympian gods.

PORSENA, Lars. Leader of the Etruscans in the sixth century B.C., when they attacked Rome to restore the Tarquins to the throne.

PRAENESTE. A town in Latium in the hills 20 miles east of Rome, famous as a summer resort.

PRIAPUS. A fertility god.

PROCULEIUS. Gaius Proculeius Varro, brother-in-law of Maecenas, who gave each of his two brothers a third of his property when theirs was lost in the civil war.

PROETUS. King of Tiryns, whose wife, Sthenoboea, when rejected by Bellerophon, accused the latter of making love to her.

PROMETHEUS. The Titan who, in Greek myth, made men from clay, stole fire for them from heaven after Zeus had forbidden it, and was punished for refusing to reveal which of Zeus's sons might overthrow him. He was chained to a rock, where a bird, an eagle or a vulture, fed daily on his liver.

PROTEUS. A god of the sea, with the power of changing his shape.

PYRRHA. She and her husband Deucalion were the sole survivors of the Deluge in Roman myth.

PYRRHUS. King of Epirus, leader of the Italian Greeks against Rome, who won costly battles in 280 and 279 B.C. The Pyrrhus of iii. 20 is a pseudonym for one of Horace's acquaintances.

PYTHAGORAS (*fl.* 540 B.C.). A Greek philosopher who taught the doctrine of the transmigration of souls. He claimed that in a previous existence he had been Euphorbus, the son of Panthous, a Trojan killed by Menelaus, and took Euphorbus' arms from the temple in Argos to emphasize his claim.

PYTHIAN. Pytho was the early name of Delphi, the town sacred to Apollo.

QUINCTIUS HIRPINUS. A friend of Horace to whom *Epistles* i. 16, is addressed.

QUINTILIUS VARUS. Critic and friend of Vergil and Horace.

RAETIA. A country between the Danube, the Rhine, and the Lech, north of the Po.

REGULUS, M. Atilius. Consul in 267 and 256 B.C., who returned voluntarily to Carthaginian captivity in 250 B.C.

REMUS. Twin brother of Romulus, killed by him after he contemptuously leaped over the wall of the city Romulus was building.

RHODOPE. A mountain in Thrace.

RHOETUS. One of the giants who attacked the Olympian gods.

Romulus. One of the twin sons of Ilia and Mars, the legendary founder and first king of Rome; in some legends, he was taken to Olympus by his father, in others he was buried in a tomb in the Forum.

Sabaea. A district in southern Arabia.

Sabine. The Sabines were a tribe in the hilly country on the border of Latium. The region was famous for its witches; its wine is inferior. The Sabine Farm given to Horace by Maecenas was about 25 miles from Rome, 7 miles from Tibur.

Sacred Way. A street that led to the temple of Vesta, the Forum, and the Capitol.

Salii. Twelve priests of Mars, guardians of the sacred shields, who performed a ritual dance every March, chanting ancient hymns, and ended their festival with a banquet.

Samos. An island in the Aegean Sea, off the coast of Asia Minor.

Saturn. An Italian god of agriculture, identified under Greek influence with Cronus, the father of Zeus, who was identified with Jupiter.

Scaurus, M. Aemilius (163–89 B.C.). Twice consul, distinguished in battle against the Cimbrians (102 B.C.).

Scopas (*fl.* 390 B.C.). A Greek sculptor.

Scythia. A territory north of the Black and Caspian Seas, inhabited by nomadic tribes.

Semele. Daughter of Cadmus, mother of Bacchus by Jove.

Septimius. A friend of Horace, recommended by him to Tiberius in *Epistles* i. 9.

Seres. The Chinese, but the word usually refers vaguely to the inhabitants of eastern Asia.

Sestius, Lucius. Consul in 23 B.C.

Silvanus. An Italian god of the forest and fields, guardian of the boundaries of farmlands.

Soracte. A mountain about 28 miles north of Rome.

Spartacus. A gladiator who led a revolt of slaves and malcontents, 73–71 B.C.

Stesichorus (*fl.* 600 B.C.). A Greek poet.

Sthenelus. In the *Iliad*, one of Diomede's men.

Subura. A street in the more disreputable part of Rome.

Sygambri. A German tribe that invaded Gaul in 16 B.C.

Syrtes. Sandbanks off the coast of North Africa.

TAENARUS. A promontory in Laconia, where there was supposed to be an entrance to the underworld.

TANAIS. A river in Scythia, now the Don.

TARENTUM. A town on the southwest coast of Calabria, founded by Spartans in 708 B.C., and sacred to Neptune. It was a resort in the Augustan age.

TARQUIN. Tarquinius Superbus, the legendary seventh king of Rome.

TARTARUS. The part of the underworld where sinners are punished, but in iii. 7 the underworld in general.

TECMESSA. The daughter of Teuthras, a king killed in battle by Ajax, son of Telamon.

TELEGONUS. Son of Ulysses and Circe, legendary founder of the town of Tusculum in Latium. He was sent by Circe to his father, and mistakenly killed him.

TEMPE. A valley in Thessaly.

TEUCER. In the *Iliad*, the great archer of the Greeks. On returning from Troy to his home in the island of Salamis, he was banished by his father, Telamon, who held him responsible for the death of his brother Ajax. He then founded the town of Salamis in Cyprus.

THALIA. The Muse of comic poetry, but referred to by Horace in a more general sense.

THURII. A prosperous town in southern Italy.

THYESTES. The brother of Atreus, who killed Thyestes' sons and served their flesh to him at a banquet.

TIBERIUS, Claudius Nero Caesar (42 B.C.–A.D. 37). Son of Tiberius Claudius Nero and Livia, stepson of Augustus, older brother of Drusus. He became emperor in A.D. 14.

TIBUR. A famous resort in Latium, 18 miles east of Rome, now called Tivoli.

TIBURNUS. Also called Tiburtus. With his brothers, Catilus and Coras, he founded the town of Tibur.

TIRIDATES. A Parthian who led an unsuccessful revolt against the king, Phraates, and came to Augustus for help in 30 B.C.

TITHONUS. Given immortality by the petition of the goddess of dawn, Aurora, who forgot to ask the gods to grant him eternal youth. He withered up until only his voice was left.

TITYOS. A giant son of Jupiter and Earth, who tried to rape Latona and was killed by Apollo and Diana.

TORQUATUS. An advocate who was a close friend of Horace.

TULLUS. (1) In iii. 8, probably the consul in 33 B.C., the year Horace received the Sabine Farm from Maecenas. (2) In iv. 7, a legendary king of Rome.

TUSCAN. The district of Etruria in northwestern Italy, and the sea off its coast.

TUSCULUM. A town in Latium, supposedly founded by Telegonus, son of Circe and Ulysses.

TYNDAREUS. Husband of Leda, who bore Castor and Pollux either to him or to Zeus.

TYPHOEUS. A hundred-headed monster who breathed fire.

USTICA. A valley near Horace's farm, in the Sabine hills.

VALGIUS, Gaius. Poet, member of Maecenas' literary group, consul in 12 B.C. None of his writings survive.

VARIUS, Lucius. An epic and tragic poet, friend of Vergil and Horace. His works have not survived, but one was a long poem on Augustus, another a tragedy about Thyestes.

VARUS. In i. 18, probably Quintilius Varus, a friend of Vergil and Horace, and the subject of i. 24.

VATICAN. The hill on the west side of the Tiber.

VENAFRUM. A resort town in Campania, near the southern border of Latium.

VENUSIA. Horace's birthplace, a town in Apulia.

VERGIL. In i. 3 and i. 24, the poet. In iv. 12, the identity is uncertain.

VESTA. Goddess of the hearth, whose sacred fire burned all year in the Temple of Vesta, near the Forum, and was renewed on March 1, the beginning of the new year. The vestals were virgins who served the goddess.

VINDELICI. A German tribe north of Raetia, south of the Danube.

VULTUR. A mountain in Apulia, near the town of Venusia where Horace was born.

XANTHUS. A river in Lycia in Asia Minor. Patara, the city devoted to Apollo, was on its banks.